Honest to Goodness Joy
7 Keys to Unlock More Than Happy

Daira Avery Traynor

Honest to Goodness Joy: 7 Keys to Unlock More Than Happy
Copyright © 2023 by Daira Avery Traynor

ISBN: 979-8-88831-010-6 Paperback
ISBN: 979-8-88831-011-3 eBook

Dallas, Texas
www.DairaTraynor.com

Printed in the United States of America.

"I have had the honor of ministering with Daira and appreciate her vulnerability and hope in encouraging others! Daira brings joy into every room, conversation, and ministry endeavor she leads. She truly lives a life of joy and I'm so glad she put her wisdom in a book for the rest of us!"

- Julia Jeffress Sadler

Next Gen Minister, First Baptist Dallas
Author of "Pray Big Things"

This one is for Alex.

Contents

PROLOGUE

PROLOGUE

THE GIRL WHO HAD EVERYTHING BUT JOY

ONCE UPON A TIME, THERE LIVED A girl who had everything. No, she didn't live in a faraway land, no magic was in the air, and the husband she had was no mythical Prince Charming. She worked hard for what she had, and her prized possessions would have been the envy of any fairytale princess. She had never in her youth imagined the thrill of driving an expensive sports car, docking a private boat, or building an estate nestled on ten acres of lakefront property, but opportunity had led her there. A passport that had seen the world and a closet full of designer shoes and trendy clothes topped her list of luxuries.

Welcome to twenty-first century living at its finest. But for this girl, extravagance left more question marks than exclamation points. While her story looked like a fairy tale everyone wanted to write themselves into, it did not have the "happily ever after" ending they would hope for. At the end of the day, a house full of empty rooms only mocked her. A designer dress accompanied her hidden tears—she was alone yet again. She had wealthy pockets but a bankrupt heart.

Who would want to listen to the privileged girl's pain as her heart broke piece by piece? Beyond the cash and material goods, she had a deep desire for a priceless item she knew couldn't be bought: joy. Her endless fake smiles, her constant chase of the next exotic vacation, and the relentless hours her husband worked deepened her gnawing conviction that this path would never produce joy. This life had become her own dead end.

THE GIRL WHO FOUND JOY

A "once upon a time" story usually ends with a "happily ever after." It's the ultimate cliché.

Spoiler alert. Life is messy, set against the backdrop of reality. You cannot predict job loss, divorce, death, or other painful experiences you go through. But you can find joy in knowing that life holds daily treasures.

Your life won't fit into a fairy tale where castles, glass slippers, and royal dances are your rewards. You can have something better than a destination that only *ends* with happiness. You can have a beautiful journey where *every* page is written through the lens of joy.

THAT GIRL WHO ONCE UPON A TIME THOUGHT SHE HAD EVERYTHING WAS ME.

I had created the illusion of a make-believe happiness, but it was far removed from the joy I truly desired. After I experienced the grief of burying my best friend, survived the aftermath of divorce, and downsized everything I owned, I finally understood what was needed: no matter what circumstances may come, joy is the greatest gift we get to unwrap.

I went on an expedition filled with unexpected twists and turns to discover honest to goodness joy. The result was seven principles that, when applied, echo out goodness. You can save yourself the heartache of living less fully than you were meant to. This book is your map. While our roads might take us to different destinations, you won't want to miss the major landmarks worth exploring!

I invite you to discover the same true joy that I now experience. Simply put, it is a joy that is honest and good. "Honest to goodness joy" is the phrase referred to throughout this book to help you see an authentic, pure joy that is yours to claim. Joy is not for an elite group; it's for everyone. Joy is your choice to make. It's an internal decision that grounds you—no matter what may come your way.

I hope you will chase after, catch, and hold on to joy. While happiness is a fleeting emotion based on external circumstances, joy does not depend on

> I hope you will chase after, catch, and hold on to joy.

your surroundings. You see, if you want to be happy, you can go to the beach. A tan and a nice drink topped with an umbrella will make you smile, but sadly, the smile will last only a short time. Beaches experience rip currents as well as sunshine. If you want joy, begin to embrace these principles one day at time. Live with confidence. Celebrate your wins. Create non-negotiables. Find fulfillment in your tribe. Discover hope even after tragedy tries to break you. The list goes on. Don't give up; tomorrow is a new day to create a life you love.

CHAPTER
ONE

1

HOT PINK CONFIDENCE

OWN WHO GOD MADE YOU TO BE

PANTS IN A SHADE OF HOT PINK

I WILL NEVER FORGET MY FAVORITE pair of pants. Far from the world of faded denim, they made a statement—a hot pink statement. You could see them from a mile away. I found them the summer before starting sixth grade. Spectacular occasions passed by all summer long, but I refused to debut them. I knew the big reveal had to be saved for my first day of middle school.

I tossed and turned the entire night before the big day. Pants ironed, backpack by the door, the perfect hair day—I was ready. The day had finally arrived. What could go wrong? I thought this bold fashion statement was my ticket in, my rise to the top of the middle school pyramid. The news was guaranteed to travel to the popular high school girls, who would think, "I can't wait until Daira joins our entourage."

It turns out that the combination of hot pink pants and a bunch of "mean girls" created a different first impression from what I had hoped for. No, it felt more like one of those slow-motion scenes from a chick flick where the girl trips down a flight of stairs before her prom date.

As I walked into class, the entire room roared in thunderous whispers. Choruses of laughter followed. Relentless nasty comments rang out, "OMG—look what Daira is wearing. Pink pants are so babyish. This is middle school, not elementary school!" Cue my exit. I darted to the nearest bathroom, trying to hide the tears. My face flushed, it became the matching accessory to my pants.

I hid in the bathroom for the rest of the day. I was desperate to go home and burn those dreadful pants—pants I had thought would give me instant popularity. I hated

those pants, and I was never going to be caught dead in them again.

When I got home from school, my mom knew better than to ask an emotional sixth grader about her first day. Dad didn't hesitate. He wanted all the details. Bring on the drama! After I shared my nightmare with him and begged to be home schooled, my dad smiled his usual grin that brightened up the whole room.

He paused, and I knew by *that* look on his face that something life changing was about to follow. His eyes sparkled with intensity as he said, "Daira, you know what you have to do? You have to wear the hot pink pants again tomorrow."

He went on to explain that it takes audacious courage to confront the noise of what others think about you. It takes tenderhearted strength to say, "I am comfortable being myself, no matter what. I like who I am."

Turns out, he was right. I really did love those pants and pink is still my favorite color. At the time, the pants expressed who I was—a middle school girl with my own sense of style. And so the next day, without hesitation, I wore the hot pink pants again.

> I am comfortable being myself, no matter what. I like who I am.

I bravely strutted through the hallways in the face of those middle school girls. How was it that just yesterday they seemed like hungry lions ready to devour me?

This time, there was silence. I walked into the classroom confidently, my head held high. And no, I wasn't rezoned to another school. I was in the same brick building, surrounded by the same familiar faces, but there was one major difference—me!

What I learned that day was that it wasn't about the hot pink pants at all—it was about owning who I was and not allowing others to change how I saw myself.

Suit Up!

If you feel as though confidence has not been your strongest suit, let's learn how to dress up together—confidently. I wonder if you have your own equivalent to my hot pink pants story. If you do, I hope it has a happy ending. I hope someone was there to affirm how special you are. Yes, you are perfectly fashioned by God. I hope a voice of encouragement reminded you to own who you are, even when bystanders threatened to compromise your uniqueness.

We all have moments that threaten to break our confidence. I call these moments "pivotal points" because, during these times, we have options. We can either allow our confidence to rise up in exceptional ways, or we can hide behind our insecurities. Joy flourishes when confidence—truly owning who you are—can be not only seen, but more importantly felt.

I used to think confidence was reserved for the select few. Of course the pretty enough, the smart enough, and the brave enough are always comfortable in their own skins—no matter what they are wearing. I wondered if I could be like them. Could the practice of "faking it until making it" be applied? I realized, though, that confidence is not an added accessory—it's who you are. I also learned I am not alone in these feelings. We all want to be truly confident, and with a little practice, we all can be.

Where do you fall on this scale? Are you confident in who you are, the unique ways God hardwired you? Or are you trapped in the chaos of middle school drama, willing to burn the hot pink pants you once loved because others have determined your worth?

I will be the first to admit that I desire to please people. When I don't feel accepted, confidence can become a struggle. I have learned, however, that at the end of the day when I'm being myself, my many quirks, flaws, and strengths blend together like oils mixed on canvas—creating my own Rembrandt. I am a work in progress that I want to own. The same is true for you. You are a work in progress, and you must own who you are. You have something beautiful to offer. Can you imagine what kind of joy you might feel if you really believed this?

If you want to experience honest to goodness joy, begin to get excited about rightfully claiming your confidence. Self-assurance is a joyful endeavor. Just like a child the night before Christmas, you are about to unwrap something epic! You are about to unwrap the person God made you to be. Confidence is a natural part of the joy process because people who are secure in how God made them cannot help but smile about it. God creates beauty. Consider all of

> You are a work in progress, and you must own who you are.

God's magnificence, from a beautiful mountainside to the intricate feathers on a bird, and know that you are at the center of what He deemed "very" good. Once this truth resonates, shouldn't your perspective on worth change? When this message sinks deeply into your heart, you can walk with joy in your step and inspire others to live in the same manner.

BE YOUR OWN FASHION STATEMENT

Climbing the stairway to confidence starts and ends with embracing what is good. This idea may seem rudimentary, but it can be daunting when we find ourselves constantly looking through a critical mirror. So often we frame our opinions around what others have distorted. Our true reflection is how God sees us. If we can begin to see ourselves in this light, framed within the context of goodness, we can live each day confidently!

What do you love about yourself? So often, we either feel guilty about embracing our good, or we feel there is a lack of goodness within ourselves. Instead of discovering the good, we gravitate toward the negative. Now, I recognize we could all make a laundry list of things we wish were different. If we have weak ankles, wearing red high heels becomes a problem. If we have straight hair, all the hairspray in the world won't hold lifelong curls! Forget the heels and the curls, own the ballet flats and straight hair, and watch how you set the next trend.

But wait . . . there's more. Swimsuit season!

How do we learn to embrace our bodies? Let's be honest—we've all experienced moments when the salty fries won over the kale salad. Although we can admit there is a time and place for both, we need to see our bodies in a different light. Don't let your thoughts about your body be the equivalent of a boxer with a punching bag. Why do we allow our bodies to make or break our confidence? To some, size zero is runway ready. To others, thousands of dollars are spent to plump up their trunk! If you are laughing at that statement, that's good! It's both true and ridiculous. We have to rise above society's harsh standards and, instead, love who we are.

Your confidence will grow when you choose to place your focus on the good. It's that simple. The more you practice this awareness, the more you will train yourself to see the good.

What you focus on, in the end, will actually be all that you are able to see. For example, have you ever noticed that as you begin to consider a vehicle (let's say a red Jeep), suddenly they seem to multiply on the road? *Were there always this many red Jeeps in my city?* The answer is yes. The difference is that now you're focused on what you choose to see—red Jeeps.

> We have to rise above society's harsh standards and, instead, love who we are.

The same is true about who you are. I challenge you to not only see the good within yourself but to also document it!

Take a moment to write down five things you like about yourself.

Keep trying. Now write down five more things you like about yourself.

This will stretch you to continue digging deeper. The more you search for your uniqueness, the more you will begin to embrace how wonderfully God fashioned you.

PACK LIGHTLY, UNLOAD THE EXTRA

It can be challenging to accept our physical qualities, but what about the thoughts we battle in our minds? What about the emotional parts of ourselves we fight with? We have to embrace every aspect of who we are if confidence is to thrive. Let's journey down this path together.

Time to pack . . . Carry-on only!

Do you carry unnecessary baggage? You know, the things you overpack that only weigh you down. Oftentimes the things that are heaviest for us to carry have to do with our emotions.

Quick story: I am a terrible packer. Going on any trip with me (even overnight) equals many suitcases packed as though I may never return. *Rain boots? Put them in the suitcase—you never know!* Well, it's all fun and games until my back breaks from the overstuffed suitcases that no longer allow the zipper to do its job. Of course, it's always the underwear that hangs out! So here, I overpacked for my trip to Europe and part of my transportation involved quickly changing trains. How did I transport two oversized bags in under a minute? At one point, I threw the bags from the platform onto the train. All eyes stared at me like one might view an exotic animal at the zoo. Why did I feel the need to bring my entire wardrobe as I went from plane to train to automobile?

The same is true with our emotions. We overpack our lives with unnecessary, negative thoughts. We hold on to things we need to let go of. And when we refuse to release these negative emotions, we wonder why we can't live joyfully. Sometimes we even invite other people to the party! Often we unknowingly give others the power to determine our emotional state. If a person isn't adding value,

> Don't give anyone the power to zap your joy.

they are subtracting it from you. Don't give anyone the power to zap your joy. Refocus on what is positive and let go of what is negative.

Another powerful joy killer is comparing our shortcomings to someone else's "perfection." Comparing will kill your joy every time. Confidence is crushed by comparison. Why are we spending hours each day on our social feeds? Why are we inserting ourselves into other people's vacations, perfect outfits, or family photos? We add layers of stress by trying to place ourselves in someone else's narrative instead of working on our own story. In the end, we only subtract from our joy. Perhaps one of the reasons we live less confidently than we should is because we think someone else's garden is more beautiful than ours. How can we compare sunflowers to roses?

Let's start packing lightly. Negative emotions and comparisons are like extra luggage that only weigh us down.

Your Best Fit (Like a Perfect Pair of Jeans)

When God created you, He saw the person you would become. He saw the good that you have yet to discover. In fact, God knew every detail needed to fashion you. You are your best fit! Are you creative—turning old furniture into trendy, vintage keepsakes? Are you great at analyzing people—turning observations into

> When God created you, he saw the person you would become.

sales? Are you a natural encourager—turning someone's tears into renewed hope? You are unique—abilities that come effortlessly to you are assets that someone else desires. Play to your strengths. Your life is a résumé, and no one else has your specific story or skill set. You bring something of value to others precisely because of your specific journey; never underestimate or devalue how amazing you are. Confidence lives in the crevices of your self-discovery.

Two Queens before the Crown

QUEEN VASHTI

"Who do they think I am?" Vashti inquired of her handmaiden.

She straightened her crown. Emerald eyes burned with intensity as she gazed in the mirror. "I am Queen," Vashti reminded herself. "Am I going to allow the king to compromise my integrity? Am I just a pretty face to be paraded around the banquet halls?"

Although Vashti continued with her line of questioning,

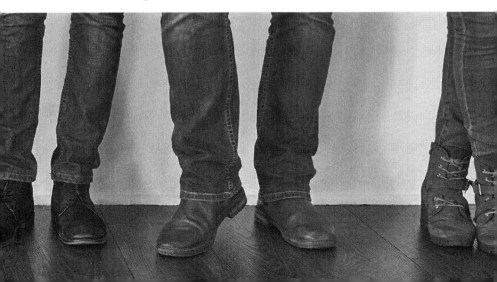

she already knew the answer. No man, woman, or even king would determine her worth.

The king and his many guests awaited her arrival. It was late into the night. Boisterous music and royal wine were in abundance. It was a feast where every pleasure was encouraged as the king sat on the throne celebrating his power and wealth. Vashti was summoned to be the highlight of the evening.

But Vashti wasn't coming.

Unafraid in her response to the king's command, she replied, "No."

She knew who she was. She knew what she was risking. She knew that, with or without the crown, she was unwilling to be taken advantage of.

As much as the king may have loved her, Vashti's act of defiance led to the king banishing her from the kingdom. Saying "no" to a king closes the door to second chances. As Vashti packed her bags, she packed all of who she was. She no longer carried the title of queen, but she never measured her confidence by the crown she wore on her head.

QUEEN ESTHER

Who do they think I am? Esther wondered. Beautiful women, one by one, paraded themselves before the king. It was a royal beauty pageant. The winner would be queen. Everyone envisioned the crown on her head—everyone, that is, except Esther.

"Orphaned" and "impoverished" were the only labels she wore. *How could a humble Jewish girl outshine all the beauty in Persia?* Certainly, this was what Esther pondered as she fell asleep. When the morning sunlight woke her, her entire world began to change.

The trumpets sounded, and Esther quickly stepped out of insignificance into nobility as the king placed the royal crown on her head.

"I am Queen," she rehearsed out loud to her handmaiden.

Her deep brown eyes gazed in the mirror. *Do they have the right girl?* She wondered.

Some of you may know how this story ends. The king

unknowingly was about to persecute Esther's people—the Jews. Would Esther remain silent or allow confidence to rise up? She would need more than confidence to accept her position as queen. Confidence would be a prerequisite to saving a nation.

Esther, once a voiceless girl, composed herself to walk into the palace and speak boldly before the king on behalf of her people. Strength rose from the same place apprehensiveness

once occupied. You may know the famous line spoken by her uncle:

ESTHER 4:14

"If you keep quiet at a time like this, deliverance and relief for the Jews will arise from some other place, but you and your relatives will die. Who knows if perhaps you were made queen for just such a time as this?"

Esther straightened her crown. I like to think she was wearing pink as she petitioned the king.

STRAIGHTEN YOUR CROWN

Esther was born to become queen and save her people. Hers is an epic story. An ordinary girl bravely uses her royal status to serve a purpose bigger than herself.

God placed this plan within her from the very beginning. The same is true for the plans He has for you. Allow God to reveal what He has already placed within you. Embrace your value and confidently move forward into your destiny.

> Allow God to reveal what he has already placed within you.

We all have Esther's courage within us, yet we all have insecurities that dare us to remain in the background instead of standing tall on the frontlines. Maybe standing up for yourself isn't proving a bunch of sixth graders wrong about your fashion choice. Maybe your calling won't find you strategically placed before a king. But you were born to be exactly who God made you to be. Stop running. Straighten your crown. Know your worth.

We also have Vashti's strength within us. She may not be highlighted as a hero in the story, but she truly was. Women's empowerment? Absolutely! She was courageous enough to own who she was and rightfully say "no" to a king. We all have the capacity to know who we are and what we will and won't stand for. If we lived this way, we would see how confidence can change our world.

YOU ARE ROYALTY

Both Queen Vashti and Queen Esther wore crowns, but their confidence moved them forward more than their crowns. You don't have to wear a crown to be confident. Allow your circumstances to create a beautiful story where you, the main character, rise up. Your joy will come alive when you know how valuable you are. After all, you were born for such a time as this!

> Your joy will come alive when you know how valuable you are.

Let this be a reminder. Confidence takes daily courage. Our physical, mental, and emotional selves depend on this strength. Sometimes it looks like saying "no." Sometimes our strength moves us forward in unexpected and remarkable ways. Let's stop comparing ourselves to others. Instead, let's take hold of our own value. If we do so, we will inspire others to rise up.

Straighten your crown, wear the pink pants, and own your confidence.

CHAPTER
TWO

2

SMALL WINS

LIVE VICTORIOUSLY ONE WIN AT A TIME

THE QUEST FOR LOUIE

"I'LL GIVE YOU FIFTY DOLLARS—that's my final offer," I asserted.

Wide eyed, I studied the room. A few other desperate shoppers were also eager to strike a deal. Somewhere on Canal Street, New York City, I had gained access to a secret room filled with fake designer bags. It was heaven on earth for a sixteen-year-old fashionista.

Everything that surrounded me was covered in plastic. I was mesmerized by the glitz of Rolex, Tiffany, Gucci, and Prada all calling out my name. Who cared if the labels were misspelled or the gold was beginning to rust? Given my limited budget, it was as authentic as I was going to get!

"OK, OK, hurry," the Asian man whispered.

One last time I carefully examined my pick of the litter, the best bag of the bunch. I had to be certain every stitch was in place. Would anyone be able to guess my Louis Vuitton was an impostor? Handing over the cold hard cash, I felt I had a winner.

I had big plans for the adventures Louie and I would embark upon. We would dine at cafés, attend movies, and shop at local boutiques where I would casually sling the bag over my shoulder like a celebrity. But two short weeks later, one of the handles on the pleather purse snapped off. My runway strut down the halls of my high school sporting the "iconic bag" was short-lived. I vowed that day, when the hot glue gun could no longer hold the bag together, that someday I would earn the right to carry the real deal.

ROUND TWO: LOUIE REVISITED

Years later, the memory of Canal Street had faded, but my quest for finding my very own Louis Vuitton hadn't. Allow me to take you on another journey, this one rather lavish. *Bonjour!* With my passport stamped "Paris," I was headed to the flagship

store of Louis Vuitton. The aroma of crepes, baguettes, and macaroons filled the city streets, but I was on a sweeter mission.

I entered through the revolving glass doors. The presence of security guards reminded me of the high cost of this mission. I heard classical music grace the ivory keys and tasted sparkling cider, its bubbles tickling my tongue.

The finest French accents inquired, *"Madame, quel sac aimeriez-vous voir* ?" (Ma'am, which bag would you like to see?)

Out of the utmost respect, sales ambassadors wore velvet gloves to handle the delicate leather, and I knew this was no longer Canal Street.

I was hyperfocused as I viewed every bag twice. I tried to dismiss the thought that with its hefty price tag, every purse should come with gold inside. Calculating the exchange rate, I justified, *At least it's tax free.* For a short moment, I was tempted to walk away. But I had made myself a promise. I had earned this win. I had found the one.

Girl meets Louie. Girl falls in love. As I danced the streets of Paris, I embraced my newfound romance. I held my head higher than the Eiffel Tower. I decided, then and there, that everyone deserves to feel this kind of joy. Everyone deserves to take the needed time to celebrate their hard work. Everyone deserves to win.

> Everyone deserves to take the needed time to celebrate their hard work.

STARTING SMALL

There is a great difference between pretending to win and earning real victories. Let me share my story, the pages between Canal Street and Paris. It comes to you by way of many, many small wins.

Seven years passed between negotiating for a fake bag in New York City and purchasing an authentic Louis Vuitton in Paris. During this time, I held on to the promise that I would someday trade pleather for a genuine leather Louie. I knew the day would come and the celebration would be joyous! The only thing that stood between me and the smoothest French leather was a few small wins.

The story begins and ends with my deep love for fashion. While I was binge watching my guilty pleasure show, *Gossip Girl,* I fell in love with a fictional character, Blair Waldorf. She quickly became my fashion icon because she wore a crown every day, as if appointing herself queen was permissible.

I was after the crown, her best accessory. Although not a royal crown, her fashionable headbands captured my attention. Unable to find her designer headbands anywhere online, I thought, *I'll craft my own.* I began wearing my original designs (inspired by the show) and the compliments began to follow. I wondered—*can I sell these?*

Free and Crowned was born shortly thereafter. I founded a company where beautiful headbands were handcrafted to make every woman feel like royalty. In addition to creating unique headbands, my greater mission was to support a cause I am passionate about: raising awareness about human trafficking. Every headband sold would give 25 percent to help eradicate sex trafficking.

Owning a company proved to be exhausting, so I celebrated as often as I could. Month after month, the company grew. I continued to design dozens and dozens of new headbands each month, never forgetting to celebrate all the "firsts" along the way.

Here are a few worthy wins:

- The first headband sold to a customer who wasn't a family member!
- The first custom flower crown I designed for a bride's wedding.
- The first time I gave a young woman, a victim of human trafficking, a headband.
- The first employee hired—I could no longer be a solo act.
- The first international sale (the idea that someone in London was wearing my design made me dance around my house!)
- The first one thousand boxes sent out.

Every first felt like a major win. Every chance I could (in between the glue-gun burns and the back-and-forth trips to the post office), I tried to celebrate.

Next came the busiest time of the year. The entire holiday season was a blur. Long hours meant little sleep as beads, bows, and buckles were scattered throughout my office. Deck the Halls with orders! I felt as if I was an elf in Santa's workshop. As I carefully crafted each headband, I tried to imagine the joy it would bring each person. With every order completed and Santa's sleigh filled, my happiness bubbled up like a bathtub filled with suds. My win could finally be claimed. As I celebrated reaching my yearly sales goal, I knew this success meant Louie and I would soon embrace. This time, no impostors would be invited to the party.

As I boarded the plane to Paris, I fastened my seat belt, knowing exactly how I planned to celebrate my win. I took a deep breath and began to savor every moment of the joy I felt. As I looked out the window and smiled, I wondered, where was Santa's sleigh and where was my new Louie?

When was the last time you made yourself a promise to celebrate? If you made a to-do list last week and checked off every box, did you reward your efforts with a tasty mocha latte? Or did you forget to acknowledge yourself? We often dismiss rewarding ourselves after reaching small goals. You might think this practice is extravagant, but why do we neglect the value of celebrating our wins? We should never wait for someone else to applaud us— we need to pat ourselves on the back. Pivotal moments need to be recognized and

> We should never wait for someone else to applaud us — we need to pat ourselves on the back.

celebrated in your life, no matter how small they start out. I assure you, celebrating will motivate you on your journey to bigger victories.

ALWAYS EAT CAKE

If you've ever witnessed your child scoring a goal on the soccer field, passing their driver's test, or getting accepted to their

dream college, you know what might follow. There is always a prize, be it an ice cream sundae, a victory dance, or a loud scream of "I did it!" Yes, reaching a goal should always be followed by a reward. Why do

we limit our times of celebration as we get older? I have learned two things: First, we need wins. Second, we need to celebrate our wins. Winning feels good and celebrating creates joy. It's why weddings, birthdays, and anniversaries matter so much to people. We want reasons to eat cake!

Winning feels good and celebrating creates joy... We want reasons to eat cake!

We were born to win. The problem? We often fall into one of three categories that stop us from winning:

1. **Forgetting to Set Goals.** If we don't set goals, measuring our wins cannot occur.

2. **Setting the Bar Too High.** We set goals that are unattainable. When we fail, we lose confidence in our ability to win.

3. **Moving on to the Next Goal.** We don't take the time to celebrate our wins. Instead, we focus on the next big thing without stopping to enjoy the value of a reward.

What category do you fall into: forgetting to set goals, setting the bar too high, or moving on to the next goal too quickly? No matter what the setback is, identify it so you can correct it. You can experience a win. You deserve to celebrate you.

Hip, Hip Hooray!

When was the last time you felt the exhilaration of "Hip, hip, hooray?" Sadly, it might be difficult to remember. Why do we skip the thrill of applause and the needed pause to take in our accomplishments? Stage performers understand the importance of this celebration. When they take their final bow, they can't help but smile. The performers understand that they successfully followed the script, and they bask in the accolades that follow. Yet in life, we often omit the curtain call.

Write out your goals and define the recognition you are going to give yourself once you reach them.

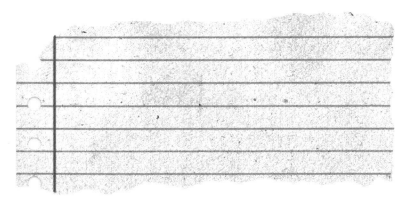

Keep in mind that defining and celebrating winning is up to each player. Does a goal that a CEO sets for her tenth year in business resemble a goal set by a first-time mother starting an online shop? Certainly not. Should they celebrate their wins anyway? Absolutely! Both are achieving amazing things that need to be given their own "Hip, hip, hooray!"

Can you name the last time you celebrated yourself? No, your birthday doesn't count. I know that if I go months without celebrating a win, no matter how small it may be, I become discouraged. Begin to find wins in all areas of your life. Look at your relationships, careers, and personal goals as exciting opportunities where you can uncover your small wins. The more you search, the more you will absolutely find reasons to celebrate. Let this choice become your lifestyle—winning

will look great on you.

Great news! Small wins launch us into greater wins. Like the small movement that causes the first domino to knock over a dozen more in its path, celebrating one small win can lead to many others. Mentally, we prepare ourselves to expect more good things to follow. Like dominoes, our energy continues to move us forward into new victories.

You might be wondering, "Why does winning come effortlessly for some, while others never get their moment in the spotlight?" I used to wonder about the winner's circle. What I discovered is that winning is a mindset. Anyone can win if they are willing to set a small goal and then celebrate when it is achieved.

Here is an example that plagues a lot of women: losing weight. Let's say you set a goal to lose twenty pounds. This number can feel overwhelming for anyone. Drinking plenty of water, going to the gym, and eating healthy are the basics that most people acknowledge as part of the journey. But let's face it, sometimes eating pizza and watching Netflix are more appealing. Sure, you're trying to lose weight, and your heart is in the right place, but can you win the battle in your mind? What if, instead of focusing on the daunting number of twenty, you focus on losing just five pounds? Maybe you give up soda? Maybe you take a walk every night? Maybe you stop snacking after 8:00 p.m.? Whatever it takes to shed five pounds, once completed you will be a quarter of the way to the larger goal!

Here's the catch. You are now five pounds lighter; it's

time to celebrate *you*. Choose a prize:

1. Fill up the tub and use that fancy glitter bath bomb.
2. Take a fun selfie and share this win with your friends online.
3. *Just do it!* Buy a pair of Nikes that will get you to the finish line!

After celebrating, do you feel motivated to keep going? Of course! Time to lose the next five pounds. Guess what? After you reach this next goal, you will be halfway there. Keep

going; small wins make it possible for bigger wins to occur. Your wins create joy. When you start to experience the benefits of winning, you will continue to challenge yourself to live in happier, healthier ways. We all have small wins within us. We simply start by setting goals that are attainable and then celebrating when they are reached.

Start by setting one goal in a specific area. Here are some ideas, although you are not limited to these suggestions: You can choose to lose weight, write a book, go back to school, or courageously sign up on a dating app. The goal can center around anything you have placed in the category of *I'll Get Around to It*. Let your "to-do list" become your "goal list." You can then move forward with a goal to win while making a few stellar changes. Map out your bench markers, each one with its own specific prize.

> We all have small wins within us.

Want to give it a try? Write down in the space below one small goal and the reward that will follow.

You will find that every celebrated win is a step forward. Learning to create a lifestyle where there are always things to achieve and celebrate on your table will increase your joy. When you see every goal as having a reward associated with it, you will be greatly motivated to continue. The best news is that your brain will associate goals with celebrations, and in the long run, you will accomplish far more than you ever thought possible.

It's that simple. Start small. You can do amazing things one victory lap at a time. I am reminded of a verse that encourages us with this very idea,

---

ZECHARIAH 4:10

"Do not despise these small beginnings, for the Lord rejoices to see the work begin."

DAVID BEFORE GOLIATH

A shepherd boy and an undefeated opponent faced each other in the ultimate battle. The odds against David did not shake his confidence as he prepared to take down Goliath. He remembered the times when he had rescued his helpless sheep from the mouths of lions and bears. He had experienced small wins in green pastures. What could prevent this win on a battlefield? With great anticipation, David inquired, "What will be done for the man who kills this giant?" The answer ignited David's passion for the win.

As he reached for five smooth stones and the sling in his pocket, David imagined the celebration that would follow. Victory meant he would be given the finest riches from the king's court and the hand of the king's daughter in marriage. David braced himself and loaded his sling as both armies watched in disbelief. He knew the battle was the Lord's and his victory would follow.

The ground shook as Goliath fell. One small stone, embedded in a giant's forehead, marked David's great win. The impossible had become possible. David basked in his army's tumultuous cheers. He had come as a shepherd boy and now emerged a champion. Worship to God and celebration couldn't help but follow. Who was this teenage boy with more guts than most men? Humbly, the giant slayer tucked his sling back in his belt and moved away from the crowds. He was already looking toward his next win.

David continued to be no stranger to small wins. Psalm after psalm, battle after battle, David juggled war, wins, and worship with a heart that longed to give God glory. Dusty caves to palace corridors, David took great delight in trusting God in every triumph he experienced.

Heartache, despair, and lament did not stop David from focusing on what was promised to him. He knew that one day he would be the king of Israel. Nothing could deter him from his destiny, and small wins paved the way. David celebrated every win by rejoicing in the Lord, knowing it would be the key

to his ultimate victory.

David allowed every season to be marked with praise, his lips declaring God's goodness over him. His circumstances mattered far less than the assurance he had in his future. Eventually, all he had hoped for came to pass. As David took his seat on the throne, oil dripped down his beard for the second time. He remembered the prophet Samuel anointing him and promising that this day would indeed come. David was victorious again. Unlike past victories in pastures or on battlefields, he was now the leader of a nation.

It had been many years since he felt the smooth pebbles against his palm. Many things had changed, yet one thing remained. From shepherd boy to king of Israel, David understood the importance of celebrating his wins.

A Recipe for Celebration: Add More Praise

I've never understood the competitive nature of sports, the sizable paychecks the players receive, or the overall love of the game. But I do appreciate and understand the need for the celebration that follows. Do I love the Big Football Showdown? You bet—I am all for the halftime show, the witty commercials, and the junk food that lures people into the party. I'll host—go team! Celebrating is a natural thing.

We should always celebrate along our journeys. More than eating a piece of cake or purchasing a designer handbag, however, rewards have the opportunity to be even greater when we choose to thank God. I encourage you to not only celebrate your wins but also praise God for them. Our willpower and determination alone are able to do extraordinary things, but when we combine our wins with God's presence, we can live victoriously every day.

Although bystanders may not understand the power behind every song sung, every instrument played, and every hand raised to the King, this worship is the highest form of celebrating. It's our response to God's faithfulness. When we celebrate our wins and show gratitude to God, He responds to us with His goodness. This is

...when we combine our wins with God's presence, we can live victoriously every day.

our ultimate win. How will you praise God for your wins? While I often do this through music, worship can also take on other forms beyond a song. We can praise God by listening to His Word, declaring His faithfulness, serving others, submitting to what He calls us to next, or giving an offering. We can choose how we worship; the most important thing is that we don't withhold praise from the One who is worthy to receive it. How will you praise God for your wins?

As a final token of love, don't beat yourself up when you fall short. Always build yourself up. You are doing great things every day. Always take time to recognize your progress, celebrate often, and praise God for the good things that will follow. You can become your biggest cheerleader. As you take on this new role, watch the joy in your life multiply. Go forward, celebrating one small win at a time.

CHAPTER
THREE

3

SETTING NON-NEGOTIABLES

CREATE BOUNDARIES THAT STICK

UNTANGLING THE MESS

HUNDREDS OF TANGLED CORDS resembling the design of an intricate spider's web lay scattered across the office floor. I stared at the impossible mess, recalling a time when I found an old jewelry box filled with rusted silver and gold chains all knotted together. I had asked myself the obvious question, "Is it worth it to separate every chain, or should I just throw them all away?" I decided then on the latter, but this situation was different.

My new boss startled me from my thoughts with his aggravation. "Daira, I want every one of these cords sorted and labeled. Don't bring me any more pie-in-the-sky ideas because there is real work to be done!"

Have I really just moved across the country for this?

A few weeks prior, I had been hopeful. I watched the moving truck haul away all my little treasures in corrugated boxes. I knew that if I bravely followed the path ahead, I would unwrap joy. From the sandy beaches in Tampa to the rush hour traffic in Dallas, I was ready for a massive change.

Welcome to my new zip code. Trading in the flip-flops for cowboy boots, I was now two weeks into my dream job. Every day, I woke up to a new nightmare. The balloons were deflated, the cake was gone, and all the well-meant congratulations were now memories in my head. The party was over. Life was heating up like the blistering temperatures outside.

Let me take you back to the beginning of how this story unfolded: I had decided after a year of restlessness that I needed a colossal change. After I made up my mind to pursue a new ministry job, I sent résumés across the country. "Let's see what happens," I fearlessly declared. Online interviews led

to airplane tickets, and I traveled to places like Kansas City, Chicago, Boston, Atlanta, and Dallas, wondering where I might end up.

I finally landed deep in the heart of Texas. I was now the head of worship and the pastor to an army of teenage students. I was so excited that I never considered, *What if something goes wrong?*

A month into my relocation, I wondered if the job could get any worse. I was eager to prove my worth, but my boss seemed even more willing to see me fail. Every day he gave me another chore. Walking his dog, fetching coffee orders for interns, and, sadly, watching my innovative ideas tossed into a trashcan became my daily routine. I was managing mundane tasks instead of leading people. While my heart knew I could do amazing things, I also knew a bird in a cage could never fly.

Later I learned that the hiring committee had interviewed hundreds of candidates for this job and had decided my skill set was a perfect match. Yet my boss was not in favor of their decision to hire a woman. I was the lightning in his storm, and he feared I might steal his thunder.

After months of tolerating the mistreatment, I caved. I called my mom in tears. "This job is a nightmare and shows no promise of changing." She conservatively reminded me that I was receiving a good paycheck. Yet I knew in my heart that this situation had crossed a line. I needed a creative work atmosphere to thrive. This principle had always been my standard, a non-negotiable that I vowed to keep. Because of this conviction, I realized I needed to immediately remedy the problem.

I walked into the human resources office and resigned. I felt lost and lied to, but I also felt empowered. I knew this decision would pave the way for a better opportunity.

ROUND TWO

This time, my non-negotiable would have to be met and my lost joy rediscovered.

Sure enough, a short time later I accepted an amazing ministry job. One of my non-negotiables, to work in a creative environment, was happily supported by all the leaders. Bonus: I even received a higher salary!

One day after work, I called my mom again. "This is my dream job. I would do this for free!" She admitted, "I never thought I'd say this, but thank God you didn't listen to me." I paused for a moment, took in what she said, and smiled. "Mom, it's because I know my non-negotiables."

NON-NEGOTIABLES: THEY'RE A BIG DEAL

Before we can fully dive into why non-negotiables matter, let's talk about negotiating in general. Have you ever negotiated for a vehicle or new home? Did you walk away thinking you got a great deal, or did you feel slightly ripped off? The idea of negotiating is that every party gives a little to get a little until all sides are satisfied with the outcome. If you are good at negotiating, you will feel you've gained something, or at minimum, held your own. But there are times when even the best of the best have to give something up.

Non-negotiables are the opposite of this concept; they are *not* up for grabs by others. Why? Because your non-negotiables are the principles you will fight for, always standing your ground. They are values you need to set because without them you give up part of who you are. You must discover what your non-negotiables are, so you can embrace them each day with conviction. Negotiating away your non-negotiables will always steal your joy.

When it comes to defining your non-negotiables, start with the basics. What are your deal breakers? What do you need to live your best life? What do you refuse to tolerate? Begin to name and list these things. Having clarity will ensure your success.

> You must discover what your non-negotiables are, so you can embrace them each day with conviction.

Coin Toss

Think about non-negotiables like a coin—they are two-sided. Let's say heads are "yes" (something you need) and tails are "no" (something you avoid).

Let's start with heads up. What is something you truly need to thrive? What is something that energizes you, even if it seems a little selfish? For example, maybe you need a weekly exercise class to reset from your busy work schedule. You should encourage yourself in this endeavor. Our bodies need care just like our minds need sharpening.

Here are some questions you might be asking:

Can a non-negotiable be a need to travel and seek adventure? Absolutely. For some, discovering exotic places is always on the agenda, something a one-day trip to the beach will never satisfy. If this passion defines your non-negotiable, don't feel guilty. But know that every choice you champion has trade-offs you must let go of. Set a budget and make it happen!

Can a non-negotiable be wanting the family to gather around the dinner table each night? Absolutely. Find new recipes and ring the dinner bell. You get to decide the things that matter most to you.

Now to the flip side of the coin. What is something you need to avoid? If you've ever said, "Never again," you may have identified something that should be a non-negotiable for you. For example, maybe you had an unhealthy relationship in which someone continually lied to you. Decide now that any relationship moving forward must be built on honesty. Set this value as an absolute—a non-negotiable that you stick to at all costs. Begin to think of your non-negotiables as specific boundaries you've set for your own empowerment. Be

selective. Your non-negotiables will test you at times. You must be prepared to champion them.

SETTING YOUR NON-NEGOTIABLES (IN STONE)

Setting non-negotiables requires dedication. If you've ever felt your life was running you instead of you running your life, it might be because you have not established your non-negotiables. Don't worry—you are not alone. I shared the story of "Untangling the Mess" because I was in the same boat that you find yourself in. I was conflicted between honoring my non-negotiable and playing it safe. I knew keeping that particular job ensured a paycheck, but it compromised my creativity and growth. We all have to make hard choices that require bravery and action. I can name dozens of coffee conversations where a friend expressed how something in her life was not right. Many times, her pain was because a non-negotiable had not been articulated and followed.

Have you ever stayed in an unhealthy situation too long because leaving would start to unravel things? Maybe you took an unhealthy job, but quitting would mean moving again. Or maybe the person you are dating treats you poorly, but moving on means you'll probably lose your mutual friends. Having non-negotiables in place will prevent this stalemate from happening to you as you navigate the difficult decisions you know you need to make. The good news is, the sooner you discover your specific non-negotiables, the sooner your life will be safeguarded from unnecessary pitfalls. Some would call this "having boundaries," but non-negotiables take this concept even further. Why? Because boundaries shift, whereas non-negotiables are set in stone so nothing can shake your foundation.

Imagine you are sitting at an oval table next to a lawyer, whom you have hired to protect your assets. Across the table is a person who has every intention of taking those possessions away from you, one by one. You meet with your lawyer knowing that a settlement means compromise. She turns to you and asks, "What are you unwilling to sacrifice? Give me a list of your non-negotiables."

Friend, while you may not be going to court, hire yourself to protect your own assets. You may be sitting across the table from an unrewarding job or an unhealthy relationship that threatens to steal your joy. I encourage you to never surrender when it comes to what you need. You will always be your best advocate.

> Non-negotiables are set in stone so nothing can shake your foundation.

ADDRESSING WHAT FEELS COMPLICATED

Let's address two concerns you may have. Here's the first: "It feels selfish to have non-negotiables." Although, I recognize that non-negotiables may feel self-indulgent, think of them as self-care instead. When you are on an airplane, you will always hear the flight attendant say, in case of an emergency landing, put on your mask first before helping others. Why is this instruction unselfish? You can't help anyone until you first rescue yourself. Simply put, you are not a selfish person for claiming a few non-negotiables that matter to you.

Here's the second concern we will address together: "What should I do when my non-negotiables appear to be impossible because of life circumstances?" I hear you. Each of our stories are complicated and can threaten our non-negotiables. In my story, I was able to leave a difficult job situation because during that period I was constantly searching and eventually able to secure a new job. If you have three children relying on you as a single mom, you might not be able to quit your job at the moment. Still, if the job robs you of your non-negotiable, you need to take steps toward a healthier solution. Update your résumé, network with others, and continually look for opportunities that move you out of your current job.

Let's consider one more factor: "What can I do when my non-negotiable involves another person's participation?" You can control only your part. You have to express what you need. If your non-negotiables have been compromised by an unhealthy relationship, you may have to forgive the person and move toward clearer boundaries. Or you may need to forgive both that person and yourself and move on without them. Only you can adjust and discern what is the right decision according to your specific situation. Don't forgo non-negotiables altogether just because your current situation is complex. Everyone has complications that threaten their non-negotiables, but those complications are exactly why you need to make non-negotiables a crucial part of your life. Non-negotiables were never meant to be suggestions that could be overturned by circumstances.

> Non-negotiables were never meant to be suggestions that could be overturned by circumstances.

Do you remember the fable of the frog in the boiling water? As the water temperature

slowly rose, the frog adjusted its body temperature accordingly. Once the water began to boil, the weakened frog could no longer jump out. He had missed his opportunity to jump while he still had the strength! Unlike the poached frog, we need to make changes before our comfort level fully sets in and our routines become permanent.

HELP WANTED? I'VE GOT YOU!

Let's discover your non-negotiables.

Here are three questions to get your wheels turning:

1. What life passions need to be satisfied?
2. What compromises have you made that you regret?
3. What bothers you more than anything else?

As you think through these questions, you will arrive at your destination—your own set of non-negotiables. It's helpful to both write and speak your non-negotiables. There is something powerful about declaring what you need. And the more you share them with others verbally, the more commitment you will feel.

I have written these three non-negotiables in stone for me:

1. A life of worship where I lead and practice it daily.
2. A creative work environment where I am achieving a goal.
3. A passionate relationship with my spouse where I feel connected.

These values come from either a place of past pain or from a place where my joy was heightened because I had the courage to put my foot down. Stop for a moment and name your non-negotiables.

After establishing this list of values, you have to protect them. They are valuable. Defend the non-negotiables you have set—you are worth it.

DANIEL BEFORE THE DEN

"I will never stop praying to my God." Daniel was unshakable. The intensity in his dark-brown eyes marked the seriousness of his conviction.

A Persian king had made a decree; the captive from Judah refused to obey.

As far as Daniel was concerned, no earthly king would ever stop him from praying. He had long ago counted the cost.

Who was this man who would dare to defy the king's order?

In the Medo-Persian empire, rumors about his greatness had traveled far and wide. Taken captive from Jerusalem as a young man, Daniel served in the royal court of the world's most powerful kingdoms: Babylon and Persia. Daniel never returned to Jerusalem, but he continued to uphold his faith in God even though pagan customs and traditions pressured him to change.

Some stood in awe of his conviction and integrity while others were filled with jealousy and rage. Yet Daniel stood strong in who he was and what he believed. Make no mistake, Daniel's eyes had seen great things. God had spoken to him through dreams and visions. In a foreign land, he had risen to one of the highest governing positions.

Daniel had learned foreign cultures and languages, yet never forgot his own. He would not be changed by what surrounded him. Why? What was Daniel's non-negotiable? To serve only the one true God, Yahweh.

Nothing will test a non-negotiable like a lion—a furious, four-hundred-and-twenty-pound carnivore who needs meat to survive. Daniel knew these cold, hard facts when he refused to adhere to the king's wishes. Was he foolish or fearless?

I propose an alternative adjective for our hero in the story.

Daniel was knowledgeable. Daniel knew two things that could not be altered. The first was his non-negotiable: to serve only the one true God, which meant daily prayer. He could not bow down to another. The second was that lions are always hungry. These two truths could have caused a great battle within his mind. When the time came for his life to be

served up for the lion's dinner, would Daniel be dead meat, or would Daniel choose to stop praying to God? Daniel's non-negotiable was stronger than the great cat's thunderous roar.

Cue a cluster of lions and Daniel's sleepover. Can you imagine this slumber party where no one was shutting their eyes to sleep? Once again, Daniel saw something miraculous. An angel shut the mouths of the lions. This was a remarkable God moment. But I wonder, could Daniel have clung to his faith and obeyed God rather than a powerful king without that non-negotiable already deep within his heart? Would Daniel's story even exist without his non-negotiable and an Almighty God?

FAITH AND NON-NEGOTIABLES

While non-negotiables no doubt affect your mental and emotional state, they also greatly affect your spiritual life. I encourage you to spend some time in prayer to determine what God might be asking you to examine within your faith. For instance, maybe you need to set aside a quiet place to meet with Him daily. Or maybe Sunday mornings need to be rededicated to going deeper into His Word. A non-negotiable in your

By knowing what you believe and allowing those values to give you strength, you can change your world with a greater impact.

belief system will help you stand stronger. When your faith is unwavering, you will find that your other non-negotiables follow with more grace.

The truth is, we can all go astray when we forget to prioritize our faith. By knowing what you believe and allowing those values to give you strength, you can change your world with a greater impact. Just like Daniel, you can stand strong in your convictions, no matter what lion you face.

WANTED: YOUR NON-NEGOTIABLES

Non-negotiables give your life the meaning your story needs to jump off the page and become noteworthy—just like Daniel. Let's carve our non-negotiables in stone, never dependent on our circumstances but engraved on our hearts, no matter what. Our faith, our relationships, and our overall joy depend on it.

CHAPTER
FOUR

4

TRIBE

FIND YOUR PEOPLE

SCENE 1: HIM (SEAN)

I will never forget this day. "HI, I'M STELLA."

As I made my way to the man dressed in plaid, his dimples made me instantly like him, something I was not prepared to admit. This was supposed to be one casual date, nothing serious. I had no idea how to reenter the dating world. A bit clueless after a painful divorce, I had decided to gradually dip my toe into the dating pool. I was in no rush to dive in. I wanted to remain in shallow waters.

But I felt as though I was in over my head, the way a student might feel when heading off to college for the first time. After all, I found Sean on a dating site, not in a Hallmark movie where happy endings are always written into the storyline. What would he think when he found out I had given him a fake name?

I paused. Who is Stella anyway? And a burner phone?

I had made myself untraceable like a person in the witness protection program. (Can you really blame me for taking extra precautions? I've watched enough *Criminal Minds* to know a handsome stranger is always a prime suspect!)

And yet, like dominoes, I fell. Piece by piece, day by day, I couldn't stop it. Like a child taking home a puppy, I had discovered a new joy, a forever best friend. I wondered, *Can I see him again and again and again?*

I dreamed.

SCENE 2: MINI-HIM (LUKE)

Captivating hazel eyes stared at me. Long, doll-like lashes blinked twice as he took in my nervous smile and the cake pop I held in my hand.

"This is for you," I said, hoping the sugar would give me the credit I needed to win over his heart.

Truth was, I had no experience with five-year-old boys. Interacting with young children was not in my youth-pastor comfort zone. Dramatic girls were my strength.

The boy squeaked, "You're my dad's new girlfriend, right?"

I smiled politely. "Yes, and I am so excited to meet you, Luke."

He paused to take in what I was saying as if he were trying to read a difficult word in a book.

Then something clicked. "Cool, let's go jump."

Just like that, we ran through the door into the trampoline park. Little did I know, this three-foot-tall boy would change my life.

We jumped.

SCENE 3: HER (EVELYN)

Perfect. This was my time to shine. My happy place. My ministry has always been to middle and high school girls. *But what if I'm wrong? What if I mess this up?* I was nervous for

a second time, much like a hopeful candidate waiting for that follow-up interview. This meeting felt as though it could make or break a career. I walked into the mall giving myself a final pep talk. *Daira, you've got this.*

I saw her. Her face looked as if it could inspire a new Disney princess. When she smiled, she had his dimples. She ran up and hugged me.

"I'm Evelyn."

Within seconds, I felt at ease. We started talking as though we had known each other for years. As we walked the mall discussing the latest fashions, I got to know the details of her twelve-going-on-twenty-year-old life. It was my version of a double espresso with whipped cream on top.

An hour later, Evelyn, Luke, Sean, and I made our way to the LEGO store. The challenge? We would try to make LEGO characters that looked exactly like each one of us. One piece at a time, like a puzzle coming into focus, we began to build something special.

Mission accomplished! Four LEGO figurines had been created, and we had all bonded.

Just when I thought it couldn't get any better, Evelyn asked, "Dad, can we buy these, please? It's the four of us, our family."

Dream. Jump. Build. One chapter at a time.

FAMILY SCENE: YOUR VERSION

Do you have a story about how you met the people you call

family? While the opening scenes of my story may have captured your attention, believe me, there is much more to write. Every story worth telling has plot twists. Every story has ups and downs, laugh-out-loud moments, and tears that have drowned out joy. The fireworks that make you fall in love with your people won't light up the sky continuously. We cannot write a perfect story because none of us are perfect. We all bring our humanity into our close circles.

Maybe you, too, have a great scene from your story. I am willing to bet, however, that difficult moments have also made an appearance—stories you will never share. Trust me, you are not alone.

People are messy, creating families who are messy, living out situations that are messy. But in the midst of the messy, true joy will remind us that beauty lives in our collections of chaos.

> But in the midst of the messy, true joy will remind us that beauty lives in our collections of chaos.

FAMILY SCENE: THEM (SOMEWHERE, USA)

The aromas of perfectly seasoned turkey, marshmallow-topped sweet potatoes, and pumpkin pies fill the entire home. Martha Stewart would be impressed. It's a holiday where gratitude is the star ingredient. The family gathers around the table set with the fine china used only once a year. Grandpa begins his lengthy prayer where even Moses is mentioned, while stomachs growl and mouths water. Then the chatter begins, and the scene takes an unexpected turn.

"Are there no vegan options?" Aunt Sunshine complains.

Suddenly, you hear more noise coming from the kitchen as dishes clash and clang, hitting the floor. Of course, Aunt Sunshine yells out, "Why didn't you use Grandma's recipe for the cranberry sauce this year?"

Next, you hear a knock at the door. It's Cousin Vinny, late again, with his annoying girlfriend.

You wonder, *Are all these people really related to me?*

You clean up their dishes for hours and no one volunteers to help. Exhausted, you ask yourself, *Would I choose these people if given the choice?* Family—for better or worse—are a part of us.

SHOULD YOU UPROOT?

Let's be honest (this can stay between us). Not every family gathering creates the joy we long for. The nostalgia found in *Full House* episodes leaves most of us wishing we could trade one of our messy family members for someone more like Uncle Jesse. The reality is most families are broken. In a world driven by technology, where every smile can be Photoshopped, we can't always see the true picture. Most families have faced difficult issues like abuse, alcoholism, depression, and abandonment. Can you relate? Is your family a place where your joy is lost or found?

There is an expression, "Blood is thicker than water." Has this saying ever been used to guilt you into thinking family relationships should be more important than all others? Just plan a wedding and you'll quickly learn how your joy drains when families make the event about everything except the bride and groom. Why does the aunt with horrible stage fright want to make a speech? Why does the mother-in-law want to be in charge of all the centerpieces when she's allergic to flowers? Why can't we just put all the guests who don't get along at the kids' table? A wedding can become utter chaos when trying to navigate all the family dynamics.

Have major events or moments in your life echoed these same sentiments? You might wonder, aren't families for comfort and guidance? Shouldn't they make tough situations easier? Don't guilt yourself into thinking drama circles only your family tree. You are not alone. As you try to respect everyone's opinions, your personal boundaries can break. Don't allow the balancing act of trying to please everyone become like trying to juggle too many balls in the air. You weren't

meant for the circus!

As you catch your breath, be encouraged that your family can be transformed into a remarkable combination of both blood and water. Yes, family members are inherited, but they can also be beautifully chosen. Let's learn together how this unique combination can become your family, or what I love to call your "tribe."

Can You Rebuild?

The people you choose to spend time with become family. They share in the little moments with you, and they create the lasting memories you savor. They can become some of your greatest sources of joy.

Families can emerge from friend groups that gather around food and laughter. They can develop from church members you know beyond the Sunday pews. They can grow through precious legal documents, when you adopt the one(s) your heart cannot live without.

The best families are the ones you choose to call your own, much as Christ chose us. Families are the people we choose to love, even when their behavior is not at its finest. Joy lives in tiny toes, prayers around fast-food dinners, and tough fights that end in *I am sorry* and *I love you*. Your people

> The best families are the ones you choose to call your own, much as Christ chose us.

can consist of everything from biological family members to blended marriages to close friendships. They are the people you belong with. They are your combination of blood and water. They are your tribe.

Your tribe shares in your stories, chapter by chapter. They are there embarrassing you on the dance floor at a wedding. They are there comforting you with another tissue at a funeral. They are there celebrating when your firstborn comes home from the hospital. They are always there. You need a tribe, a place to belong. You need your family!

YOUR TRIBE

Life is filled with ordinary events that can take us on unforgettable journeys—dreams come true, jumping can be exhilarating, and building can create masterpieces. As life unfolds, we are led to the extraordinary people that complete us. Our tribe comes together as our daily life is lived out, one story at a time.

Good news! There are over seven billion people on our planet to choose from, and you only need a handful to create joy. The odds are in your favor. If you had asked me years ago about my tribe, my answer couldn't have been complete because I didn't know the beauty that awaited me. It may be the same for you. You may still be in search of your people, or you may already know who your tribe is. Either way, trust that God has people for you. Be on the lookout for them and remain patient. God could add anyone to your life, at any time.

Discovering your tribe is a personal journey. The people you will someday call your tribe might be found on a dating app, a chance meeting at a coffee shop, or through an RSVP you almost passed on.

We all need a place to belong. Get excited about the future. As you make a commitment to this search, you will find that joy is best experienced in the company of others. Be motivated by all the laughter, memories, and friendships that will form because of an initial hello.

If you need an extra boost of confidence before you step out, here's an acronym I created and use often, with five key actions words to keep in mind, based on the word *TRIBE*:

T — **Trust.** Trust God will bring you the right people.
R — **Release.** Release unhealthy relationships.
I — **Initiate.** Make the first move.
B — **Belong.** Take your rightful spot.
E — **Expand.** Don't limit the future.

Take a moment and think through the information given after each letter in the word *TRIBE*. Notice each letter requires a move on your part. Which action is the hardest for you? How will you begin to overcome this fear?

Write it here:

Your difficult action word (based on **TRIBE**):

Your next steps (how you will overcome):

As you remember to *trust* God, allow yourself to *release* anyone who is not meant to be part of your tribe (you will know when someone is not working). Releasing that person means letting them go. A hard conversation might have to take place, followed by forgiveness, so you can move

Allow God to move in unexpected ways by taking the first step. Take joy in belonging to your tribe, claiming it as your own.

on without bitterness. Then, *initiate* new relationships. Allow God to move in unexpected ways by taking the first step. Take joy in *belonging* to your tribe, claiming it as your own. Tribes hold joy, safety, and love within them. They are a gift. Likewise, never close the door on the future. The ways in which you *expand* your tribe could change your life, as only God knows what awaits you. Be faithful and allow God to build something special, a family that grows deep roots.

NAOMI BEFORE RESTORATION

SCENE 1: THE WIDOW (NAOMI)

Strands of gray hairs had multiplied, too many now to count. Streams of tears fell, uncontrolled, like weeds in her former garden. Nothing was left in her that was not overgrown by sorrow and despair. Her name was Naomi, but she called herself Mara, which means "bitter." The name change would show the world her truth. The person she used to be was gone. Her heart was buried in the grave along with her sons and husband. She was a nomad without a place to call home.

SCENE 2: THE DAUGHTER-IN-LAW (RUTH)

Ruth followed an unlikely leader. Her allegiance to Naomi, an aging outcast, was remarkable. There was no logical reason for Ruth's loyalty, but she followed Naomi like an inescapable shadow. Ruth's life followed no plan. Tomorrow held no certainty. But Ruth didn't focus too much on the future. She saw only the present. She clung to the hope she saw in Naomi.

NAOMI & RUTH: A TRIBE OF TWO

I've always wondered what Naomi was like before she met her loyal daughter-in-law. Could her life have been complete without Ruth?

Although most of the book of Ruth details the two of them together, Naomi's life began quite differently. She thrived with a husband and two sons before a famine sent them from Bethlehem to Moab.

From that point, Naomi's story became one of grieving, as she suffered many losses. First her husband died. Then her two grown sons. She resolved to go it alone, in solitude, back to her homeland, but someone decided to follow—Ruth. Little did Naomi know that Ruth was the daughter-in-law who would change the course of history.

The more I study this story, the more questions spiral

in my mind. I have come to believe that history is rich with details I will never fully know. This, of course, makes me love the story that much more as my imagination runs wild with hypotheses. Something beautiful must have led up to this famous moment:

RUTH 1:16

But Ruth replied, "Don't ask me to leave you and turn back. Wherever you go, I will go; wherever you live, I will live. Your people will be my people, and your God will be my God."

As I read this Bible story, it brings me back to the events that defined my own story. You see, because I understand the power of dreaming, the courage of jumping, and the completeness of building, I can't help but cheer Ruth on. This was Ruth's journey of dreaming, jumping, and building a unique tribe with Naomi. They must have walked hundreds of miles on dusty roads while Naomi grieved.

Why did Ruth desperately want to follow her? Why did Ruth love her? What made Ruth's loyalty to her unfettered? Ruth stayed through the bad, the worse, and the ugliest of times. Did Ruth see something we didn't get to witness? Yes.

Ruth saw God within Naomi, even when Naomi could no longer see him.

As their story unfolds, we see God creating a special tribe. Ruth married Naomi's relative, Boaz, a man of great wealth. The marriage created a rebirth of joy for Naomi. A child would be born, making Ruth a mother and Naomi a grandmother. Yet there is far more to this story than a new family being established—God's hand is on every page.

Generations would hear Ruth and Naomi's story. More dreams would come to fruition as a shepherd boy became king. Yes, King David could trace his ancestry back to these women. And as David's deep roots continued to grow, something else was birthed. Hope was placed in the lap of a world through another child from this lineage: a baby born in Bethlehem called Emmanuel, meaning "God with us."

Because Ruth followed Naomi, we can follow the lineage of this small tribe of two to the birth of the Messiah, Jesus Christ. Truly, the limitless wealth of this story will require all eternity to uncover. How could Ruth's bold declaration to serve Naomi's God, Yahweh, result in her adoption into the most significant family the world would ever know?

Naomi and Ruth were family, but not by blood. Regardless of their humble beginnings, God had a plan for their lives that exceeded all expectations. They were a tribe of two, divinely expanded into many.

Ruth and Naomi's story never ceases to give me goosebumps. It is a remarkable story where the most unlikely persons take center stage. Ruth trusted the unknown. She released all her past ties. Ruth initiated the journey. She chose to belong. Ruth's faithfulness expanded God's plan for her life. This is the power of a tribe.

TRIBES MATTER

We crave meaning so we try to look to the past for answers. We search for little clues, hoping we can better understand our stories with the evidence we uncover. We begin a journey to discover the *greats* in our family heritages. We walk down the path to find out who our ancestors were, only to encounter potholes along the way. We desperately want to understand our pasts, but do they necessarily change the futures God wants to write within us?

When I visited Ellis Island, I became intrigued with my family roots. I wondered if the people who lived before me had accomplished extraordinary things. Did my Italian ancestors bake the first pizza? Were they Renaissance musicians or famous artists? Unfortunately, most of my questions about their legacies are still unanswered. My quest to find greatness in my past was unrealized. I am happy to drop my search and let those inquiries remain in the past.

Will you join me? The answers for our futures cannot be found solely by looking into our pasts. What if everything depends on the choices we are making right now? Focus on the joy created by your tribe today and watch your future flourish. If Ruth and Naomi had focused on their pasts, they would have clung to loss and grief. Instead, their present was what God used. He destined the two women to change the future.

Your tribe, however big or small, is God's gift to you. They are the people who will change your future. Who knows, their impact may even be far greater than what meets the eye. Your family might be blended, like mine. Your tribe might include adoption, in the manner that Ruth was brought into the family of God. Your people might belong through both blood and water. Cherish your people, belong to your tribe, and share your unique story with the generations that follow.

> Your tribe, however big or small, is God's gift to you.

Your tribe matters. Each person contains treasure within. God is writing the story of our families, and there joy is found. Go ahead, dream, jump, and build today. You are paving the way for a beautiful tomorrow.

CHAPTER
FIVE

5

THE GOLDEN GIFT

DISCOVER THE VALUE OF GIVING

THE BIRTHDAY GIFT

I was surviving my own teenage version of *Groundhog Day*. For what felt like many months, I was in the same story. I was like a runner on a treadmill going nowhere. While my closest friends were out buying the latest boy-band shirts, I was with my mom on a never-ending shopping trip. Like babysitting the screaming kids next door, this was a new form of adolescent torture!

Let me describe the scene for you. My mom and I would go through the side entrance of the mall, past the food court and the aroma of Cinnabon, to a popular store that had become my foe. Mom asked the question again, "Daira, which one? The champagne gold has a classic feel, but the icy blue and the rich lavender are beautiful as well. Which one should I pick?"

I wished the answer I gave would result in a final decision. Could this please end in the swiping of plastic, the carrying out of a package wrapped in a bow? If only I could help my mother decide on the right color of pen.

The words "Sensa pen" will forever stay with me like indelible ink. My mom had wanted one of these expensive pens ever since the first time she held the silky gel texture of its barrel between her fingers. She said the way these particular pens wrote was equivalent to pouring melted butter on lobster. I might have had more luck, however, purchasing a winning lottery ticket than she had walking away with the pen in hand. The issue? These pens were around a hundred dollars a pop, and even though we could afford it, my mom never spent money on herself, especially on something as lavish as a pen.

So when her birthday came around, the celebration didn't look like chocolate cake, a string of balloons, or wrapped presents. No, instead we presented her with (drum roll, please) a gift card to the iconic store! This would be the day when my mom would go to the famous store and walk out with a Sensa pen. Then, we would all celebrate. I was nominated to ensure this mission went according to plan.

After several trips back and forth to the register, we finally had a winner. It was the champagne Sensa pen. She had gone for the gold like an Olympic champion! I will never forget *that* look on my mom's face as she handed over the gift

card—part guilt and part bliss.

Fast forward, and less than a week later, my mom and I arrived at her all-time favorite place—our church. It was a place where songs like "Amazing Grace" and sermons on love were celebrated. We found our way to our usual seats and felt at home. As we sat down, a lady with a feathered hat smiled and made her way next to us. I had never seen her before, but she seemed at ease, not like the typical visitor who hoped no one would notice them.

It was time for the offering portion of the service, and my mom carefully took her Sensa pen out of the case. I noticed the lady with the feathered hat glancing our way. There was nothing unusual in my mind as my mom wrote out her check. She had always been a faithful and joyful giver.

When the service ended, the lady with the feathered hat began to chat with my mom. I don't remember a word that was said until the lady commented, "I was admiring your beautiful pen during the offering. I love Sensa pens, but I could never afford one." I assumed this conversation would be lengthy, as my mom would tell our great tale of purchasing the birthday pen. But instead, my mom smiled, reached into her purse, handed over her beloved pen and said, "God bless you!"

I wanted to scream as I followed my mom out the front doors of the church. The lady with the feathered hat now owned the prized pen. What did I miss? All of these questions flashed before me: *Mom, do you have a fever? Did you just give away the pen that shaved months off my life? Is my Groundhog Day about to reset . . . again?* Selfishly, I was missing the whole point.

When we reached the church parking lot, tears rolled down my cheeks. "Mom, why? Why did you just do that?"

She responded with more joy than the day she bought the pen. "Daira, we should never hold on to anything too tightly, even the things we love. God blesses us so we can bless others."

That day, I took home more than just the words of a sermon. Imprinted in my mind was my mom's joy in action. While this event occurred over twenty years ago, its emotional impact has never weakened for me. By now, it's possible that pen is lost or out of ink. But the choice to give it away makes the pen and its lesson live on forever.

Years later, as an adult, I bought my mom another Sensa pen with a note, "God blesses us so we can bless others." Thank you, Mom, for the joy I saw in your giving.

> God blesses us so we can bless others.

JOYFUL GIVING

What does true, authentic giving look like to you? Giving with no strings attached, no "thank you" needed, and the willingness to do it all over again, is genuine giving at its finest. Oftentimes we only give because we expect something back. Like throwing a boomerang, we hope giving comes back to us in the same manner. Have you ever found yourself thinking in this way? *I will buy you a wedding, birthday, or baby shower gift, as long as you are willing to do the same for my celebrations.* Yet there are no expectations when giving is a selfless act. This type of giving will open doors to joy because it comes from the heart and is not determined by another person's response.

Presents on repeat! Let's talk about Christmas, because I will use any excuse to talk about the holidays. "It's the Most Wonderful Time of the Year," "Deck the Halls," and "We Wish You a Merry Christmas." While carolers sing familiar tunes, we sip hot cocoa, trying to wrap our stress in a nice

bow. If we are honest, maybe the holiday season feels more like "Grandma Got Run Over by a Reindeer." Jammed parking lots, long lines at the registers, and maxed out credit cards do not make the season jolly. Let's face it, we don't always give presents joyfully.

Confession time: I dread buying presents, especially when December rolls around. Yes, it's the holiday season and I'm making a list, checking it twice. Why doesn't it even matter if they were naughty or nice? The long list of people I need to buy presents for always leaves me with the same emotion: *Is this really necessary?* It's not because I'm cheap or because I don't like to shop (anyone who knows me would call my bluff on that one!) The reason I dislike presents for "everyone on the list" is that it feels more required than desired. It appears like a swap—you buy me something and I will buy you something. Best case? The gifts are a success and we don't need the gift receipts. It is exhausting. Joy from presents? It is more like the ultimate buzz kill. That's when I started to discover that presents and gifts are very different.

GIFTS VS. PRESENTS

Instead of learning how to give gifts, we buy lots and lots of presents—presents that overflow under our pine-scented trees at Christmas and end up being sold at garage sales in the spring. You might be wondering then, what is the alternative? Coal? Bah humbug?

I propose that, instead of buying presents, we should

focus on giving authentic gifts. A gift is not the same as a present. It is not measured by the price tag or the brand—it is, in and of itself, invaluable. A gift comes from a deeper place and costs us more. It is our time, our love, and our resources that allow us to reap the joy that comes with the sacrifice. A gift allows us to invest. A gift has deep meaning, offering something we cherish to someone God allows us to love. If we practice giving gifts instead of buying presents, we begin to see how our hearts make room for joy that bursts out into our daily lives. "Joy to the World!" When I started giving gifts instead of presents, I felt a joy I had never known before.

> A gift is not the same as a present. It is not measured by the price tag or the brand—it is, in and of itself, invaluable.

Learning how to give gifts (instead of presents) takes practice. The story of my mom giving away her Sensa pen could have been replaced with a dozen other stories I have witnessed. Often strangers, just like friends, reaped beloved gifts of kindness. How do we get to that authentic level of giving? The words might fall nicely on the page, making the action of giving seem easy, but how do we consistently practice selflessness at any given opportunity?

THE MELODY OF GIVING

There is a verse in the Bible that has always puzzled me.

MATTHEW 6:3

"But when you give to someone in need, don't let your left hand know what your right hand is doing."

When I first stumbled across this verse, I didn't give it much thought. But as years passed, I found myself reading it again and again, wondering what it truly meant.

One day I was teaching a student his weekly piano lesson. He was a beginner when he started under my wing, but he quickly proved a prodigy. The music he could play was so advanced, I began to practice for *his* lessons. He had flawless technique. I watched as he played almost effortlessly. He amazed me by the different rhythms and notes he produced simultaneously. How was he not making any mistakes? How was he processing the music on the page so quickly?

Eventually I got the courage to ask this eight-year-old boy exactly how he was doing *that*. He smiled and said, "I practice the difficult part in one hand so many times that it's automatic. I practice until the other hand has no idea what the difficult hand is doing!"

Instantly, I thought of the verse in Matthew. Could

giving be like practicing the piano? Could giving be like my eight-year-old student who practiced until he no longer thought about what his two hands were doing? Giving hands operate perfectly and simultaneously when we don't overthink. In fact, just like music, our giving is most beautifully heard when played from the heart.

> Giving hands operate perfectly and simultaneously when we don't overthink

Giving is a lot like learning to play a difficult piano piece. It takes practice for two hands to play different melodies. Our giving is no exception; our hands have to learn how to respond when giving opportunities arise. My mom played the generosity piano like a virtuoso. Sometimes, her left hand had no idea what her right hand was doing! I want to play the piano until it rings out like *that*, making the practice of giving a beautiful masterpiece.

THE WIDOW BEFORE THE OFFERING

She was unnoticeable. Like a hand wearing a glove, she left no trace. Who was she? No one really knew. No one really cared. No eyes ever gazed upon her until this particular day.

The temple was busy and the who's who had made their presence known. As the crowds came, she found herself being pushed along among the carelessness and commotion. Yet, this woman seemed unbothered.

Nameless—her identity is concealed in the Gospels of both Mark and Luke. A woman who knew how to keep to herself. Even though her sandals were worn, she had never left the outskirts of her small town. Yet her life journey had taken her far past the miles she had walked. Yes, she had stories. Yes, she had pain. To most, it seemed as though she had lost more than she gained.

As she made her way to the treasury, she decided to give away all she had left. This holy place was where she felt she belonged. Giving was her greatest joy. Her tattered garments should have created a distance between her and the others, a reason for her to feel unwelcomed, but she quickly made her way past the silk robes of the nobility. Two coins jingled in her pocket. She moved forward. Sacrifice. She lived each letter that spelled out the word.

She placed the two small coins from her pocket into the treasury. It was all she had. No one was looking. No one except Jesus, who knew every detail of her story, every tear she had cried, and all the heartache she had hidden from the

world. Jesus saw what she had given and decided the story of this woman's priceless gift would become a page in history.

AN UNNAMED WOMAN AT **IHOP**

Another round of Groundhog Day. Each night was the same. After kissing her kids goodbye, the single mom headed into work, the usual late shift. The money she earned barely covered the increasing pile of bills. She wondered if there was a better way to make ends meet. She tied her apron around her waist and noticed the growing number of syrup stains from the dozens of stacked pancakes she had served. Another exhausting shift filled with patrons who thought it acceptable to tip less than the standard percentage. "Another day, another dollar," she reminded herself.

"Excuse me, miss."

She responded to this title as if it were the name given to her on her birth certificate.

"When you have a moment, could I see a menu?"

She quickly grabbed the cleanest menu from the stack and hurried to his table, placing it before him. She noticed his casual polo shirt and jeans, but also the way he carried himself: he seemed unassumingly important. She made small talk with him as he placed his order—black decaf coffee, three scrambled eggs, and a side of extra-crisp toast. He ate quietly, and after finishing his last sip of coffee, asked for the bill.

She set the ticket next to his glass of water and cleared his plate, taking it to the dish station. When she returned, he had already gotten up to leave and was making his way to the door. She spied a hundred-dollar bill neatly folded on the table. His seven-dollar meal would surely merit change, she thought. In a hurry, she chased him.

"Sir, sir, I have your change."

He responded kindly, "No, I am not missing anything. What is on the table is yours."

Shocked, her forehead revealed new wrinkles as she desperately tried to think of a response. Instead, she stood there speechless.

He continued, "I know a hundred dollars won't change your life, but please accept it, as this gift changes mine."

That night, for the first time in a while, she felt that someone truly saw her.

FROM THE BOTTOM OF MY HEART

Giving shares no resemblance to buying presents. My mom, the man at IHOP, and the widow at the temple all knew the value of joyful giving. Each of them made an investment in a stranger's life. They had no agenda. Creating a lifestyle of giving is far more rewarding than buying a one-

> When we learn to give freely as opportunities arise, we create impact.

time present. Some of the most joyful people I know, regardless of how much or little is in their bank account, are the people who have made giving a habit. When we learn to give freely as opportunities arise, we create impact. We leave behind a mark, a legacy beyond the initial sacrifice, which God always sees, honors, and multiplies. Be inspired; giving is a worthy endeavor. Honest to goodness joy can be found when we give with an open hand, holding nothing back. I pray you can say, "From the bottom of my heart, I have learned the joy of giving."

HONEST TO GOODNESS JOY

CHAPTER
SIX

6

BLEACHED WHITE HOPE

SURVIVE TRAGEDY AND CLAIM GOD'S GRACE

HER NAME WAS ALEX

As I stared in the mirror, my skin turned paler than the hotel's bleached white sheets. I trembled in disbelief. I couldn't even process my agony.

I had planned for a serene getaway to finalize the last round of edits for this book. My celebration turned into unthinkable sorrow. Joy was erased instantly by one phone call.

I started braiding my hair. *Why? Why am I braiding my hair like an elementary school girl getting ready for her class photo? Is this what a person does when they try to avoid what is happening? One phone call, how could it change my entire life?*

"Daira, I have some terrible news," my best friend's mother had said as she sobbed. "Alex passed away last night."

In disbelief, I managed to mutter some words of condolences, then I hung up the phone call. The only thing

I could think to do at that moment was to call Alex. I had to talk to her. It wasn't until I heard her voicemail that reality set in—this nightmare was one I could not awaken from.

She was always my first call. The first person to know everything.

She was there the first day of many dramatic unknowns: my high school years. She was there when the tears flowed: my boyfriend had broken my heart—again. She was there when my life spun out of control: my parents were getting a divorce. She was there when I learned how to really pray: my driver's test. She was there for my most difficult goodbyes: I was moving out of state. She was there when I got married: my "I Do." She was there for my shame and fear of the future: the road down

my own painful divorce. She was always there, like a freckle that defines a friendly face. She was constant.

Our stories could fill their own novel on joy. Laughter with Alex was like trying to catch your breath after being underwater for too long. Friendship with her was like watching *When Harry Met Sally* over and over again, because you never get tired of the classic film. Happiness with her was like listening to "Let It Be" by The Beatles on replay, because a great melody lasts the test of time.

Every New York pizza, we devoured together. Every Broadway show, we applauded together. Every late-night drive, we cruised together. We were inseparable, attached, always together, like a teenage girl and her iPhone. I didn't know how to not call her. It didn't matter if it was a trivial thing, like seeing an ice cream truck, or a monumental thing, like my marriage falling apart, she was my first call. Alex always picked up. She was always there.

Rewind. Just twenty-four hours earlier, Alex had wished me the usual "Happy Birthday, Poodles." Rewind twenty-four hours before that, and I had encountered a haunting thought. Can a book on joy be complete without a chapter on tragedy?

Why had I expressed those words out loud? Tragedy? Why did a book on joy have to include pain? This seemed as nonsensical to me as giving an excited child a toy without batteries included! Why, deep in my soul, did I feel you needed to know joy included heartache? As I sat down to write on "suffering," I kept hitting delete. Much like a tortured artist surrounded by crumbled papers, I decided I was wrong. I didn't need "a downer" chapter because *I'm the joy girl*.

A week later, I flew back to New York and saw her lifeless body lying in the casket. This was really happening. Hundreds of people sobbing. I held the hands of her parents as they buried their only child. I laid a red rose on her grave, its petals soon to be bleached white by the strong sunlight. What could cause such vibrant beauty to fade? Some things in life will never make sense on this side of heaven.

> I laid a red rose on her grave, its petals soon to be bleached white by the strong sunlight.

It has been two years since I said goodbye to Alex, one of my greatest loves. And truth is, sometimes I still need to come up for air.

The book you are holding stayed tucked away in a file on my desktop. My life had taken so many unexpected turns that I wondered if I would ever have the courage to finish what I had started. Better yet, would I be brave enough to share her with you? Could I write this nightmare of mine permanently in ink against the white-bleached paper?

"You must start somewhere," I told myself.

So today, wherever you are, we can start together. We must.

WHERE DO WE START?

You need to hear this chapter on tragedy because it can produce hope. No one is exempt from pain. No one can escape the "hard stuff," no matter how we try. None of us can live joyfully on the mountaintop without also living in the unfathomable valley. We all have had or will have a tragedy plague our lives in an unexpected way. I cringe as I type this, but I know it is true.

Here is a spoiler for you: lasting joy is impossible without Christ's strength. How can we experience joy when we are surrounded by pain? Honestly, some people remain in their pain forever and nothing breaks my heart more. If pain is sharper than a sword prepared for battle, what is hope? Hope allows joy to sustain our hearts, even when pain pierces through.

BLEACH

Is it just me, or does it seem like every time you wear white, a stain decides to show up to the party unannounced? You didn't think making that Italian red sauce would be an issue until it bubbled up and splashed all over you. Suddenly your perfect white tank top is sporting polka dots. Perhaps you didn't anticipate your toddler's tantrum at the arts and crafts store, but now you have glitter all over the aisle and on your favorite white jeans. Nothing like leaving a sparkle everywhere you go! Does anyone else have a love/hate relationship with wearing this color?

We like things to look clean. White creates space,

even on the pages of a book. White creates an illusion that everything has been sanitized. In fact, I have a white kitchen, and it is rather obvious when I forgo cleaning. Therefore, I have concluded that the color white is an impossible shade to maintain. How many people regret buying that beautiful white couch?

Yet we have a solution! Bleach. If the color white is our foe, bleach is our bestie. In the summer when I want to show off my tan with a contrasting white shirt, I make sure a magical stain-eraser is nearby at all times. Stain, bleach. Spot, bleach. Spill, bleach. The pattern repeats.

We bleach our sheets, socks, T-shirts, and other white clothing items to make them look clean again. But how do we bleach our lives when they become stained by sin, tragedy, or unspeakable pain? There is a hymn I grew up singing called, "Nothing but the Blood." I am singing the words as I type:

> **What can wash away my sin?**
> **Nothing but the blood of Jesus.**
> **What can make me whole again?**
> **Nothing but the blood of Jesus.**
> **Oh, precious is the flow**
> **That makes me white as snow,**
> **No other fount I know,**
> **Nothing but the blood of Jesus.**

The conclusion of this song is the very point of this chapter: hope emerges from tragedy. Blood makes us clean.

I have a confession to make. I grow very faint when I think about the sight of blood. Watching gory movies makes me turn my head and cringe. I find nothing more tragic than knowing someone's death meant blood was spilled. But our greatest source of hope, the greatest love story ever told, cannot exist without blood. Throughout the entire Old Testament, the shedding of innocent blood meant a sacrifice was being offered for the cleansing of sin. Death and life still follow this cycle. We see it best when we see the cross.

A MEETING WITH GOD

I've been really angry with God. The kind of anger where you say things you never should. I have questioned His purpose and plans for me more than I would care to admit. In some

ways, I acted on pride, thinking I knew better. And I have had my fair share of doubts. In my darkest seasons, I have even felt abandoned. But I have never denied who He was. I recognize this has been a gift.

I fell in love with Jesus before I even knew what adult love would be like. I experienced real love at a time when my smile meant all sorts of missing teeth. I am thankful I met not just a man in a book, but a Savior. I was attending a Christmas drama at church where the story of Jesus was brought to life. As the play ended, I turned to mom and said, "Did the baby really die for me? I have to meet him." Without warning, I ran to the stage with joy and wonder; I wanted to know Jesus.

YOUR MEETING PLACE

If you are hurting, my heart weeps with you. If you have experienced unthinkable pain, I cannot fix it, and chances are, neither can you. I know only one permanent solution—you have to meet Jesus. Therapy, money, denial, or any other remedy you choose won't create the hope that, in the end, is available to you. In fact, I have been there, done that. I've tried the therapy sessions where you process all of your emotions—sometimes it was

> Therapy, money, denial, or any other remedy you choose won't create the hope that, in the end, is available to you.

helpful, sometimes uneventful. I've tried spending money on trendy clothes, beautiful shoes, and luxurious vacations to counter the increasing void that was inside. I've even tried denial—you know, the denial that occurs when you face the mirror and wonder if your joy can come back from the grave. I've metaphorically tried to bleach my life, my own way, with my own solutions. The truth? It doesn't last.

We can't fix ourselves when we are broken. We aren't cliché puzzle pieces. We can't create the same picture that once existed before the tragedy hit. Yet God always gives us hope. He is our new beginning, washing our past stains and tears clean. This is why this chapter is not called "Bleached White Tragedy" but "Bleached White Hope." Even when our lives experience pain, God can meet us where we are. He gives beauty for ashes and hope for despair.

START HERE

Have you ever heard the expression "Time heals all wounds?" Sadly, time doesn't move quickly enough when you are hurting. And time was never meant to fully recover what you lost. Instead, let me take you to the only place in time where complete healing occurred. A time and place where someone else's wounds created healing and wholeness for you.

Consider starting here, at the foot of the cross where love met your darkest day. It is the most complex yet beautiful place to find the healing and restoration you need. Who can understand your specific pain? Jesus. He is the only one. The truth is that when we experience unthinkable pain, we often forget to factor in that Jesus is there. We picture ourselves without the grace that is going before us. Jesus carries the weight. Scripture reminds us that He physically bore the weight of the cross, the promise of our only real hope. Who can change your suffering into a story, your pain into a new promise, and your deepest wounds into beautiful healing? Nothing but the blood of Jesus that was already spilled at a certain time and place. Calvary marked your hope. The greatest day of innocent suffering provided a way for you to go from stained to bleached—white as snow.

JESUS BEFORE THE CROSS

The air was crisp. Olive trees provided shade in the garden as tears fell on holy ground. The sky had turned from sapphire blue to complete darkness. Abandoned. Sweat turned to drops of crimson blood as He cried out,

> ## LUKE 22:42
> "Father, if you are willing, please take this cup of suffering away from me. Yet I want your will to be done, not mine."

As the words left His lips, He knew there was no other way.

There was no other sacrifice that could be made. He was the Lamb the prophets foretold. Jesus knew that surrendering to this plan meant suffering awaited him.

Rewind. Just twenty-four hours earlier, Jesus broke bread with His disciples. Now these same men were fast asleep and unaware of what was coming. The last meal they shared was marked by laughter among friends. Yet betrayal was hidden in the darkness as thirty pieces of silver were exchanged. Forgiveness was already poured out. Denial was on the horizon for when roosters would crow. Mercy had already covered it. Grace was at the table. The same grace that would endure forty lashes tearing apart skin, all the while knowing the worst was still to come. He would wear a crown of the sharpest thorns. The nails in His hands and feet would pierce and scar. The cross that would convict an innocent man purchased our freedom. Suffering. Rejection. Death. Healing. Wholeness. Life. How can this be? Bleached.

As the last words were spoken, "It is finished," the world awaited hope.

THIS HOPE

The hope I want you to claim cannot be given to you by anyone other than Jesus. It cannot be found in any self-help book. It cannot be found in the finest things the world might present to you. The only way we can survive our suffering is by accepting the cross, knowing that joy comes in the morning. Friend, I don't know what morning will look like for you or what caused the mourning that has broken your heart. Yet I know hope awaits you. Each and every day since my best friend passed away, I have had the opportunity to do the very same thing you can do. Meet Jesus and accept the cross. You, just like me, can recognize the truth that our pain was never meant to be carried alone. Jesus is right there with you, not just a man, but a Savior. Hebrews reminds us of the unthinkable—pain turned to joy:

HEBREWS 12:2

"We do this by keeping our eyes on Jesus, the champion who initiates and perfects our faith. Because of the joy awaiting him, he endured the cross, disregarding its shame. Now he is seated in the place of honor beside God's throne."

Neither pain, nor suffering, nor your ultimate low can hinder you from the honest to goodness joy I have shared with you throughout this book. Suffering leads to hope and even joy.

Although I never anticipated my story would include great loss, I see how God is using it. My joy? I know this absence is not the end. This is not my final goodbye to Alex. I don't have to fix myself. The cross already paid the price. I don't have to bleach my life from a stain I cannot clean. Jesus already finished it. You have

> The cross already paid the price. I don't have to bleach my life from a stain I cannot clean. Jesus already finished it.

access to the same truth. You can experience joy, even after your greatest storm. This hope is unlike anything else—I promise. Joy comes in the morning.

CHAPTER
SEVEN

7

BRIDGE MOMENTS

LEAP WITH FAITH TO WHAT'S NEXT

To Cross or Not to Cross?

I was somewhere in the jungle of Costa Rica where zero bars displayed on my phone. I was as remote as one could be, and I wondered, *How do I change this channel?* I was on an adventure far outside of my comfort zone, something I've only ever seen on television. Unprepared in heels and surrounded by camouflage, I tried to steady myself.

"Great," I remarked, "All that's missing is Tarzan. Why am I even here? I didn't sign a waiver for this!"

There I stood on rickety boards in front of my greatest fear. I couldn't locate the ground. I am absolutely terrified of heights, and I felt as if I was looking down the barrel of my own gun. A mile-long bridge, dangerously suspended in the air, awaited me like a death walk. As far as I could see, this bridge had no end in sight. I began to wonder if Indiana Jones would have given *this* bridge a try. This was my worst nightmare coming to life—even my slightest breath could cause the bridge to swing. High above the treetops, I had no exit strategy.

Disclaimer: normally I'm not this big of a wimp. Fears that easily paralyze others, I bravely face head on. I can confidently laugh with the creepiest of clowns. I can calmly speak in front of massive crowds. Yes, I can even carefully assist spiders back to nature. But heights, oh heights—just dangle my feet and watch me tremble.

When it comes to adventures, I envy people who are adrenaline junkies. I prefer relaxed vacations, not explorations that leave you breathless from fear. Yes, I am the bask-in-the-sun, eat-scrumptious-seafood, and shop-for-trendy-trinkets kind of a girl. I would much rather leave the death-defying quests to the superheroes who seem to have extra lives to spare.

As the tour guide asked me once again to join the group, I begged for other options. I wondered, *How hard would it be to arrange a helicopter?* Destination, anywhere but here. Yet I knew I was out of dramatic tears and reasons to announce, "Please, just permanently forward my mail here." I had to cross the bridge. There was simply no other way to get to the other side.

It felt as if I had passed out and my body was floating across the clouds. The only sound I could hear was the beating of my heart echoing louder than the boisterous monkeys below. I closed my eyes tightly, trying to pretend it was only a dream. But then, suddenly, I was jolted back to the reality that every

step mattered. The key to not falling through the frightening four-inch gaps that revealed the great drop below? Less panic, more focus, and tremendous faith that this was not my final hour.

Finally, my feet returned to solid ground. I felt the gratitude a fisherman might have after being caught in a violent storm and safely returning to shore. I fell to the ground in exhaustion from my journey and burst into tears. *I could have died!*

As I was brushing the dust off my clothes, the tour guide reappeared. He approached me hesitantly, "Congratulations, you're halfway there. At the end of today's journey, there's a beautiful waterfall. We have only one more bridge to cross."

DEFINING THE BRIDGE

My terrifying Costa Rica experience evolved from a fear of an actual bridge. But most of the time, the things we need to conquer are not literal bridges. Our bridge moments, like my suspended bridge, require our bravery. Bridges need our action and should never be ignored. Bridges connect where we are to where we need to go. Often, bridge moments are opportunities that

> Often, bridge moments are opportunities that present themselves to us, daring us to leave what is comfortable behind.

present themselves to us, daring us to leave what is comfortable behind. Truthfully, a bridge moment might be terrifying. The dilemma? If we choose not to cross, we remain stagnant. Yet if we successfully cross a bridge, we open up our lives to new possibilities that didn't exist before.

What bridge, if crossed, would dramatically change your life for the better? Defining the bridge (whatever it may be for you) is the first brave step toward your exciting future.

YOUR BRIDGE MOMENT

When was the last time you experienced a bridge moment? Did it terrify you? Did you choose to cross it, or did you retreat? My hunch is that the bridges you bravely crossed empowered you. When we conquer our bridge moments, we look fear in the face. When we push ourselves past what is comfortable, we discover how resilient we are. Playing it safe will never reap the same rewards. Yes, joy can be experienced best through the adventures we choose to take. Risk will always be a part of the ride.

BRIDGING THE GAP

You might be wondering why you need to cross the bridge moments in your life. Couldn't your joy just continue to grow while you sit on your couch? Unfortunately, no. We were made for adventures. We were made to take risks. This is why some people willingly jump out of planes and actually pay to do so. This is why some people take their hard-earned money and play the stock market. This is why some people relocate to a foreign country for a new job opportunity. We need to challenge ourselves. Who knows what might be found on the other side of the challenge? The reward and the joy that await you will be worth it.

So what stops us? We have been conditioned to choose the path of least resistance. We are conflicted between our desire for new thrills and our safety nets. You may wonder, *Is letting go a worthy endeavor? Who wants to seek out bravery when staying safe is a viable option?* You are not alone in your thinking—I used to feel the same way. But I discovered that staying landlocked kept my life on pause, while stepping into the unknown gave me the opportunity to grow. Letting go of your fears and

embracing the future is exhilarating.

I assure you, pressing "start" on your next adventure will never be a mistake, if only you know where to begin. If you feel stuck, as we all do from time to time, I wonder if you are challenging your feet. Let me explain. Are you pushing yourself enough to risk what is comfortable for what might be remarkable?

Bravery always starts with a step. For couples wanting to adopt, a step might be to start the paperwork. For a graduate wanting a job, a step might be to create an amazing résumé. For a single person wanting a relationship, a step might be to sign up for a dating site. All things, both legendary and ordinary, start with a single step.

No one understands the progress of a step like a first-time parent. As a baby goes from crawling to standing, they cross a bridge. The first step causes great joy, and no matter how many times the child falls, the bravery that lies within picks them up again. The same is true with our steps. We rise, we fall, and we continue moving forward because we simply cannot get to the other side without movement.

> We rise, we fall, and we continue moving forward because we simply cannot get to the other side without movement.

KEEP ON TREKKING!

We all are going places! Maybe

your passport hasn't been stamped with exotic destinations, but you have an exciting journey ahead of you. We all have a point A that leads to a beautiful point B. However, a bridge is often required to get from where we are to where we need to be. This is where fear can become a factor. What do we do with our fears? We must start with small acts of bravery. Of course, this bravery is always put into action by small steps.

I want to stop here for a second and allow us to breathe. Bridges are scary and so is change. Go ahead and give yourself credit for continuing on the road because so many people never dare to risk for a reward. OK let's keep trekking.

I often ask myself three key questions as an inventory check when it comes to braving my bridge moments. I challenge you to ask yourself these same questions:

1. Do I voluntarily leap enough in my life?

   YES or NO

2. Do I bravely bounce back?

   YES or NO

3. Do I take risks that require faith?

   YES or NO

As you ponder these questions, can I be your tour guide for a moment and offer you good news? Crossing bridges may leave you breathless, but the joy you will feel when you allow yourself to be brave will be unexplainable. Let's start with the first question.

DO YOU VOLUNTARILY LEAP ENOUGH?

Sometimes you just have to leap, but you don't have to do this while blindfolded. You have the ability and the resources to prepare yourself for what lies ahead. Let preparation give you encouragement, knowing that in the end, nothing will take the place of that first step. If we had the opportunity to interview Neil Armstrong, what would he say about the importance of stepping out? Would he describe the years of preparation, or would he simply focus on the need to leap? His words are iconic. Many Americans know them by heart: "That's one small step for man, one giant leap for mankind." It's the leap that was heard around the world. Yet I wondered why he chose those specific words. After doing a little research, I discovered the famous one-liner was actually misunderstood.

What was the actual statement made? *"That's one small step for a man, one giant leap for mankind."* This may not seem like a major change, but the added "a" before the word *man* completely changes the meaning. While many people contributed to the mission, only one man, Neil Armstrong, made that initial step on uncharted territory.

Likewise, you have a journey only you can take. Your footprint is needed for your specific mission. With this path in mind, you can volunteer to take that first step and allow the world around you to be shaped by your contribution.

Do You Bravely Bounce Back?

We all have the spirit of resilience within us that allows us to fall, fail, and rise again. Let me define this spirit for you. Resilience is *the capacity to recover quickly from difficulties—toughness.* You are tough! How do I know this without ever meeting you or hearing your story? Because I know life is tough, and you are braving it every day.

Keep going. Step by step, just like putting one wobbly foot in front of another on a swinging bridge, you will learn how to face tough challenges. Build resilience like a relationship with a best friend, knowing that the more you invest, the more unbreakable it

Challenge yourself to stretch, like a rubber band. You will not break.

becomes. Challenge yourself to stretch, like a rubber band. You will not break.

I would be lying, however, if I didn't admit that sometimes tough challenges have a tough outcome. What if we leap and fail?

Let's address this fear. Have you ever tried to be brave, and the outcome was rejection? Have you ever given 100 percent only to be met with disappointment? How do you keep going? How do you keep these moments from getting the best of you? I've been there. In fact, there were times when my resilience was greatly threatened. My failures mocked me.

I encourage you to reset. The sooner, the better! I love that the word *resilience* starts with the Latin prefix *re-* meaning again and again. This is what you need to do—start over again.

If you are going to be tough, as I know you are, you have to learn to release what causes you to feel weak. Toughness comes when you release what you were never meant to hold on to. Your failures, mistakes, shortcomings, and disappointments belong in the past. Discover the beauty of catch and release. Catch the lessons learned and release what you could not control. You deserve to move on.

One final thought on catch and release. I'm not much of a fisherman, but the concept of catch and release fishing fascinates me. What is the benefit of fishing all day and releasing each fish you catch back into the water? Is it just the sport of that tug on your line that you celebrate as victory? How is leaving the lake without dinner helping anyone? We can ask ourselves the same questions. Is every time you fail worth casting the line again? It certainly is. Being resilient even when there is no immediate victory allows us to grow. Be like a fisherman who just enjoys the sport of putting forth the effort. Catch the lessons learned and release the mistakes. Don't focus too heavily on the outcome. Catch and release—it's all part of the challenge. Go fish!

DO YOU TAKE RISKS THAT REQUIRE FAITH?

How does your faith play into your willingness to take risks? Faith allows you to be bold, and boldness allows you to take actionable steps even when you can't see the outcome. Faith affords you the opportunity to believe you will reach the other side. The Bible reminds us in Hebrews 11:6 that without faith, it is impossible to please God. We must act and exercise our faith. Like a muscle, faith must be developed. This is how we push ourselves to the next level.

> Faith affords you the opportunity to believe you will reach the other side.

I work with teenagers, and one thing is a given: teenage boys want to impress teenage girls. So what do they do? They join a gym. They believe muscles are the quickest way to attract a girl, and they are willing to sweat for it. As they repeat their exercise routine day after day, progress comes slowly. But fast forward an entire summer and suddenly scrawny Carter is sporting a tank top with a set of guns. Yes, the work paid off!

The same is true with our faith. We have to practice it daily to see results. Building our faith cannot be achieved at the gym. Instead, we build our faith in the quiet moments we spend alone with God. Consistency is the key. We have to be willing to spend daily time with God in prayer and in the reading of His Word. Day by day, week by week, we build up our trust that God is with us. Then we feel empowered to practice our faith and see results—results often recognized by others. The process of gaining muscle is similar to the process of developing our faith, as both require daily dedication. When was the last time you flexed? Bridge moments always require actionable steps, resilience to reset, and faith.

PETER BEFORE JESUS

MATTHEW 4:19

"Come, follow me, and I will show you how to fish for people!"

Jesus, the one everyone was talking about, stood on the bank of the Sea of Galilee. He had purposefully called out to Peter and his brother Andrew, who were a short distance away in their boat.

The invitation had been given, and an RSVP would need to follow. There would be so much to this story, an unfolding of events that would take many chapters to write. But at that moment, time stood still. How did Peter process such an invitation? Did he speculate about what following Him would be like? I imagine he wondered how a rugged fisherman could leave his boat and fish for men instead. Surely he had more questions than answers. Could he cross the short distance from his boat to the one called Jesus?

Peter stood up from the comfort of his boat—everything he knew surrounded him. A fisher of men was never something he envisioned as part of his story. As far back as he could remember, he was brought up in the family business. He was familiar with boats, fishing nets, and the sea. Who was the one who remained quietly on the shore, the one whose invitation challenged Peter to rethink the life that had already been mapped out for him?

There was something about Jesus that drew Peter in. He wanted to follow, but where would they go? Why was a simple fisherman needed for the journey? Peter knew risking everything could leave him with nothing. Could he be all in?

Peter knew that a decision to follow Jesus would change his life forever. Jesus saw that if Peter followed, other lives would be changed for eternity.

PETER KNEW ONLY HIS PRESENT CIRCUMSTANCES.
JESUS SAW THE FUTURE THAT AWAITED HIM.

PETER KNEW LEAVING WOULD MEAN EMPTY FISHING NETS.
JESUS SAW THE FEEDING OF FIVE THOUSAND.

PETER KNEW THE SAFETY OF HIS BOAT.
JESUS SAW HIM WALKING ON THE WATER.

PETER KNEW HIS FORMER DREAMS WOULD HAVE TO DIE.
JESUS SAW HIM THERE AS THE DEAD WERE RAISED TO LIFE.

PETER COULDN'T SEE ALL THAT WAS AHEAD OF HIM.
JESUS ALREADY KNEW IT FULLY.

Peter faced a bridge moment that, once crossed, would lead to his greatest adventure. He chose to leave everything and follow. Scripture gives us no hint of hesitation. It was a very brief bridge moment, a short crossing from a boat to the arms of Jesus. So many more bridge moments would follow. Peter would journey and learn from the Master. He would follow Jesus and witness a sea of miracles, as blind eyes were opened, lepers were healed, and the lame walked again.

Peter bravely crossed a bridge, and what awaited him on the other side would build the foundations of the Christian faith. He witnessed the resurrection of Jesus, His ascension into heaven, and the coming of the Holy Spirit at Pentecost. And, as was once promised, Peter became a pillar of the early church, a great fisher of men.

READY, SET, CROSS

Bridge moments are meant to challenge your feet, allow you to bounce back, and push your faith past its comfortable boundaries. It's time to make the changes you've been avoiding. Scary bridge moments are often pivotal moments that God uses to interweave His story with ours. I wonder what you might be missing out on if you choose the path of least resistance. Remember, God has a specific destination for you, and it is bigger than your current fears! Bridge moments become opportunities to trust Him instead of relying solely on your efforts.

Your bridge moments are going to be epic, and it all starts with a step. Imagine the joy you will feel when you accomplish the things you were meant to achieve. It's time to prepare for the adventures you will take. Activate your faith daily and remember that every journey you embark upon will require action, bravery, and faith. Go ahead and step out—you were meant to cross your next bridge.

CHAPTER
EIGHT

8

JOURNALING YOUR JOY

MOVE FORWARD IN JOY

LET'S MAKE A MAP

My collection of self-help books expands constantly. But can I confess something? Even after I have read all these inspiring books, valuable information remains unused on the bookshelf. You see, after I turn the final page, there is no clear roadmap to assist me in navigating from point A (the old me) to point B (the new me). A gap grows between what inspired me in the book and what actually gets applied to my life. Even after highlighting and thinking through the author's points, I need direction. If you benefit from any form of navigational system while driving, you know there is great value in a step-by-step approach to finding your destination.

Here's the deal: I don't want that situation to be our story with joy. I don't want your joy to be optional. I want your joy to last longer than the pages of this book. I want you to easily apply these concepts as you continue to journal your joy. I know life can be filled with distractions and to-do lists, so I wanted to make this process easy for you.

But first, I'm going to share a quick story at my own expense. It involves a map that went slightly wrong.

THE MAP CRISIS (CIRCA 2008)

I looked down at the directions I had penciled out for myself. My hodgepodge notes of left and right turns based on stylish window displays made perfect sense to me.

When I had arrived in Florence, Italy, for my semester abroad with no car, phone, or ability to speak Italian past obvious words like *cappuccino* and *ravioli*, I knew I had to improvise to get around. Embarrassingly, since I couldn't read an old-fashioned map, the first week of classes were a no-show for me. Instead, I spent too much time sampling gelato and savoring pasta dishes. As guilt set in, I knew I needed to create a map I could actually follow.

My map was a masterpiece complete with quirky directions and darling diagrams:

Turn right at the yellow building. When you see the window displaying all the stiletto heels, turn right again. Continue until you see the window with the rose gold leather clutch (**don't be tempted to buy it**). Just turn left and continue to follow the smell of espresso. Keep going! Turn right at the lavender dress.

The crumpled page serving as my map looked unorthodox in its presentation. But as I walked the unfamiliar streets in Florence from my apartment to the university, there were no glitches for a whole month. We were a power couple as we walked hand in hand.

Then one day, I saw the familiar words on my map, "Turn right at the lavender dress," but for the first time ever, I was perplexed. *Where is that lavender dress?* My homemade map had failed me. I was alone on the streets of Florence with no "recalculating" option.

My frustration growing, I wondered where that dress had gone. *Did it slip itself off the mannequin and decide to explore the city? Is it sick of feeling locked up?* All my questions led to one conclusion: I needed that fashionable landmark to survive the city.

It took me a while to realize that fashion changes with the season, and so do window displays! My map became obsolete every time something sold from a store window.

That day, I found myself starting all over again. Never learning to read an actual map—and no desire to start now—left me with very few options. What did I do? I bet you can guess. I reworked my map:

Turn right at the red wool coat.

YOUR UNIQUE MAP

Together, let's work on creating a unique map that leads to daily joy. You may have to rework your map from time to time to suit your needs, but that's OK. This is your map, and I want it to serve you well.

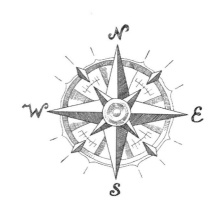

Here we go! Let's take it one day at a time as we map out the seven principles learned in this book.

THE MAP: JOURNALING YOUR JOY

Instead of trying to master all seven principles at once, let's break it down. Just imagine if every day you focused on only one principle for more joy and continued this habit for a month, six months, or a year. What would starting every Monday with confidence produce? What if every Wednesday you celebrated a win? Could this routine transform your growth and leave you smiling, a daily dose of joy? It sure could. In fact, if you

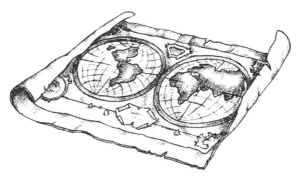

celebrated a Wednesday win for a full year, you would have celebrated yourself fifty-two times (and this celebration goes far beyond your birthday or anniversary). As you commit to this process day by day, your joy will multiply.

Here's what your daily principle focus might look like:

Monday Motivation: **CONFIDENCE**

Tuesday Tribe: **FAMILY**

Wednesday Wins: **VICTORY**

Thursday Thrills: **BRIDGES**

Friday Focus: **NON-NEGOTIABLES**

Saturday Smiles: **GIVING**

Sunday Shift: **HOPE**

The next pages will walk you through daily reflection, journaling, and actions that over time will lead you to more joy. You can use the worksheets in the book, copy them to make your own journal workbook, or download a set of PDF worksheets from my website, www.DairaTraynor.com. As you continue on your journey, I pray you discover a welling up and overflowing of honest to goodness joy.

BONUS

WORKBOOK & JOURNAL

**SCAN THIS QR CODE TO ACCESS THE FREE
ONLINE WORKBOOK & JOURNAL**

WWW.DAIRATRAYNOR.COM/WB1

MONDAY

MONDAY

MONDAY

MONDAY

MONDAY

MONDAY

MONDAY

MONDAY

MONDAY

MONDAY

MONDAY

CONFIDENCE

MONDAY

MONDAY

MONDAY

MONDAY

MONDAY

MODIVATION: CONFIDENCE

L et's face it, Mondays might rank as your least favorite day of the week. After the excitement of the weekend, Monday's alarm clock can feel downright rude. There's a reason why "Monday Motivation" has become popular on social platforms. Yes, it's time to motivate yourself with true confidence, the kind that will last the whole week.

MONDAY MOTIVATION: CONFIDENCE

Climbing the stairway to confidence starts and ends with embracing what is good.

WHAT DID YOU LEARN FROM CHAPTER ONE, "HOT PINK CONFIDENCE?"

_____

_____

_____

_____

_____

_____

_____

_____

_____

_____

_____

_____

_____ ♛ _____

When it comes to confidence, it's time to rise up. You have something good to offer others. You are valuable. You are wonderfully made. You are worthy. How do you begin to act as the confident daughter of the King? You must find your identity in Christ. Time to straighten your crown!

WHERE WOULD YOU FALL ON A SCALE FROM 1-10 WHEN MEASURING YOUR LEVEL OF CONFIDENCE? ("1" BEING YOU WANT TO HIDE BEHIND A ROCK AND "10" BEING YOU CAN ROCK A RUNAWAY) EXPLAIN WHY YOU FEEL THIS WAY.

_____

_____

_____

_____

_____

_____

_____

_____

_____

MONDAY MOTIVATION: CONFIDENCE

Climbing the stairway to confidence starts and ends with embracing what is good.

NAME THREE UNIQUE WAYS GOD HAS HARDWIRED YOU.

_____

_____

_____

_____

_____

_____

_____

_____

_____

_____

_____

♛

FOCUS ON THE GOOD. REMEMBER THE ANALOGY ABOUT SEEING RED JEEPS? YOU'RE ALWAYS GOING TO SEE MORE OF WHAT YOU ARE LOOKING FOR. WRITE DOWN ALL OF THE GOOD THINGS THAT YOU WILL CHOOSE TO FOCUS ON.

Monday Motivation: Confidence

Climbing the stairway to confidence starts and ends with embracing what is good.

It's simple. Comparing will kill your joy every time. Who do you compare yourself to? Take a few minutes to journal on how you will stop this practice. Warning, this may mean you have to limit your social media intake!

_____

_____

_____

_____

_____

_____

_____

_____

_____

_____ ♕ _____

IN THE BIBLE STORY ABOUT QUEEN VASHTI AND QUEEN ESTHER, WHO DO YOU RELATE TO MORE AND WHY?

_____

_____

_____

_____

_____

_____

HOW MIGHT GOD BE ASKING YOU TO RISE UP?

_____

_____

_____

_____

_____

_____

_____

_____

MONDAY MOTIVATION: CONFIDENCE

Climbing the stairway to confidence starts and ends with embracing what is good.

How to master this thing called Monday? Suit up! It's important to consider all areas of your life to maximize your confidence. Let's take an inventory check on your physical, mental, emotional, spiritual and social wellness.

PHYSICAL. You may not like what you see in the mirror, but embrace what is good. Likewise, treat your body kindly. See the beautiful person God created when He made you.

WRITE DOWN THREE OF THE PHYSICAL QUALITIES YOU LIKE MOST ABOUT YOURSELF.

_____

_____

_____

_____

_____

_____

_____ ♛ _____

Monday Motivation: Confidence

Climbing the stairway to confidence starts and ends with embracing what is good.

Mental. What you think matters. Know your roadblocks and what causes you to stumble. Allow positive words to sink into your soul and learn to dismiss all the lies you are tempted to believe about yourself. Straighten your crown and celebrate your worth.

Fill in the blank, I am confident because… Write down as many statements as you can think of.

_____

_____

_____

_____

_____

_____

_____

_____

_____

_____

_____

_____

_____

_____

_____

_____

_____

_____

_____

_____

_____

_____

_____

_____

_____

_____ ♛ _____

Monday Motivation: Confidence

Climbing the stairway to confidence starts and ends with embracing what is good.

Emotional. What you feel matters. Remember, when you overpack your emotions, you are creating a load that is too heavy to carry. Confidence crumbles when you allow your negative feelings to run the show. Stop comparing your garden to someone else's. Allow your emotions to be healthy so confidence can flourish.

Write down a lie you once believed about yourself that you will no longer choose to believe.

MONDAY MOTIVATION: CONFIDENCE

Climbing the stairway to confidence starts and ends with embracing what is good.

SPIRITUAL. If you have said hurtful words about yourself and believed those lies, it's time to forgive yourself. You are a child of God. You have the amazing privilege of approaching Him as "Abba, Father." Bask in who you are and let go of who you are not. Remember, you are a masterpiece, fearfully and wonderfully made.

WRITE DOWN SOME TRUTHS THAT GOD HAS SPOKEN ABOUT YOU THROUGH HIS WORD.

_____

_____

_____

_____

_____

_____

_____

MONDAY MOTIVATION: CONFIDENCE

*Climbing the stairway to confidence starts and ends with
embracing what is good.*

SOCIAL. Being confident means you are comfortable in your own skin. Do you hide parts of yourself when you are in social settings? Do you shy away from the unique things that make you quirky and fun? It's time to embrace, without apology, who you are in every 'hello' be it with strangers or friends.

YOU WERE BORN TO STAND OUT! (YES, EVEN YOU THE INTROVERT!) WRITE DOWN WHAT MAKES YOU UNIQUE FROM ALL THE OTHER PEOPLE IN A GROUP.

_____

_____

_____

_____

_____

_____

_____

Physical:
BUILD YOUR PHYSICAL CONFIDENCE.

PICK ONE.

☐ One green thing is a good thing!

☐ Wear fun shoes.

☐ Put on full makeup and style your hair.

☐ Go to the gym.

☐ Take a bubble bath.

Mental:
BUILD YOUR MENTAL CONFIDENCE.

PICK ONE.

☐ Refrain from social media for a day.

☐ Watch a Ted Talk or listen to an encouraging podcast.

☐ List five positive things about yourself on sticky notes.

☐ Forgive someone who said something unkind.

☐ Finish the sentence, "I am beautiful because…" Repeat at breakfast, lunch and dinner.

Emotional:
BUILD YOUR EMOTIONAL CONFIDENCE.

PICK ONE.

☐ Call a friend who can affirm you.

☐ Do something you are good at.

☐ Journal about yourself (positive thoughts only).

☐ Write down what feels ugly and put a line through it.

☐ Name one person you need to stop comparing yourself to.

Spiritual:

BUILD YOUR SPIRITUAL CONFIDENCE.

PICK ONE.

☐ Forgive yourself.

☐ Ask God for more confidence.

☐ Read a devotion or blog.

☐ Worship in your car.

☐ Read Psalm 139:13–14. (NLT)
"You made all the delicate, inner parts of my body and knit me together in my mother's womb. Thank you for making me so wonderfully complex! Your workmanship is marvelous—how well I know it."

Social:

BUILD YOUR SOCIAL CONFIDENCE.

PICK ONE.

☐ Text a friend and tell them how awesome they are.

☐ Compliment a stranger.

☐ Spend time with a confident person.

☐ Smile (yes, practice smiling all day).

☐ Write a kind social media post about a friend.

Monday Motivation

TUESDAY

TUESDAY

TUESDAY

TUESDAY

TUESDAY

TUESDAY

TUESDAY

TUESDAY

TUESDAY

TUESDAY

TUESDAY

TRIBE

TUESDAY

TUESDAY

TUESDAY

TUESDAY

TUESDAY

TRIBE: FAMILY

Your tribe is one of your greatest gifts. They play a huge part in your level of joy. Don't take them for granted. Commit your Tuesdays to your tribe. Remember the acronym TRIBE as you go through today's exercise.

T — **Trust.** Trust God will bring you the right people.

R — **Release.** Release unhealthy relationships.

I — **Initiate.** Make the first move.

B — **Belong.** Take your rightful spot.

E — **Expand.** Don't limit the future.

TUESDAY TRIBE: FAMILY

Your tribe, however big or small, is God's gift to you. They are the people who will change your future.

WHAT DID YOU LEARN FROM CHAPTER FOUR, "TRIBE?"

Your tribe are the people God has given you. They are the people you cry with and they are the people you laugh with. Discovering the right people will bring you endless joy. How do you find the right people and release the wrong people? Let's dive in together to create your dream tribe.

NAME SOME OF THE PEOPLE IN YOUR TRIBE. DESCRIBE WHAT YOU LOVE ABOUT EACH OF THEM.

TUESDAY TRIBE: FAMILY

Your tribe, however big or small, is God's gift to you. They are the people who will change your future.

IN YOUR OWN WORDS, DEFINE THE WORD "FAMILY."

_____

_____

_____

_____

_____

_____

_____

_____

_____

_____

_____

_____

_____

REFLECT ON THE ACRONYM FOR TRIBE. WHICH LETTER DO YOU NEED TO FOCUS ON THE MOST AND WHY?

TUESDAY TRIBE: FAMILY

Your tribe, however big or small, is God's gift to you. They are the people who will change your future.

AS YOU READ RUTH AND NAOMI'S STORY, WHAT INSPIRES YOU? HOW DO YOU RELATE TO THESE WOMEN?

_____

_____

_____

_____

_____

_____

_____

_____

_____

_____

_____

_____

DESCRIBE THE LEGACY YOU WANT TO LEAVE. WHAT ADJECTIVES DO YOU HOPE PEOPLE WILL USE TO DESCRIBE YOU?

Tuesday Tribe: Family

Your tribe, however big or small, is God's gift to you. They are the people who will change your future.

Physical. The best way to invest in your tribe is to spend time with them. Texting just isn't the same! Being with the people you love is good for the soul and will create special memories. So, get together and continue to write your stories, chapter by chapter.

Write down how you will become more intentional in getting people together in the same room! Describe what this would look like for your friends and family.

_____

_____

_____

_____

_____

_____

_____

_____

_____

_____

_____

_____

_____

_____

_____

_____

_____

_____

_____

_____

_____

_____

_____

TUESDAY TRIBE: FAMILY

Your tribe, however big or small, is God's gift to you. They are the people who will change your future.

MENTAL. Make Tuesday a day where you make a conscious effort to think about your people. Who are you thankful for? How can you serve the ones God has given you?

HOW WILL YOU BECOME MORE AWARE OF WHAT THE PEOPLE IN YOUR TRIBE NEED?

_____

_____

_____

_____

_____

_____

_____

_____

_____

Tuesday Tribe: Family

Your tribe, however big or small, is God's gift to you. They are the people who will change your future.

Emotional. Supporting your tribe means uplifting them in every season. If the ones you love live far away, call them. If your people happen to live with you, spend quality time with them. Ask your tribe what is causing them joy and what is causing them pain. Take time to talk about the hard stuff today.

What are some questions you can ask your tribe members that will lead to heartfelt conversations?

Tuesday Tribe: Family

Your tribe, however big or small, is God's gift to you. They are the people who will change your future.

Spiritual. Nothing can take the place of prayer. Will you commit to pray for the ones you love most? Ask God to protect, bless and intervene for your people. Prayer is your greatest weapon!

Write down a prayer for someone in your tribe.

_____

_____

_____

_____

_____

_____

_____

_____

_____

TUESDAY TRIBE: FAMILY

Your tribe, however big or small, is God's gift to you. They are the people who will change your future.

SOCIAL. Get excited. Allow Tuesday to be a day of searching for new tribe members. Expand your tribe! Has someone been on your heart that you could reach out to? Set a date with them on Tuesday (even if the date is later in the week). Good news, God has an important person to add to your life.

HOW WILL YOU REACH OUT TO SOMEONE NEW THROUGH A SIMPLE INVITATION? WHO WILL YOU ASK AND WHERE WILL YOU GO?

_____

_____

_____

_____

_____

_____

_____

TUESDAY TRIBE

PICK ONE:

- [ ] Work on a project together.
- [ ] Watch and discuss a movie with the tribe.
- [ ] Go on a walk together.
- [ ] Have a date night.
- [ ] Cook a meal together.

Physical:

Build Up Your Tribe Physically

Build Up Your Tribe Mentally

PICK ONE:

- [ ] Identify all your tribe members.
- [ ] List why you are thankful for each tribe member.
- [ ] Write one activity you can do with a specific tribe member.
- [ ] Set your phone background to a tribe member.
- [ ] Name five people you can reach out to.

Mental:

PICK ONE:

- ☐ Give a hug.
- ☐ Tell your tribe why they are special.
- ☐ Say "good job" to everyone in your tribe.
- ☐ Have a hard conversation.
- ☐ Release someone who is unhealthy.

Emotional:

Build Up Your Tribe Emotionally

PICK ONE:

- ☐ Ask God for new tribe members.
- ☐ Pray for your tribe everyday.
- ☐ Forgive a negative action of a tribe member.
- ☐ Dedicate your tribe to God.
- ☐ Read 1 Corinthians 15:33.
  Do not be misled: "Bad company corrupts good character." (NIV)

Build Up Your Tribe Spiritually

Spiritual:

PICK ONE:

- ☐ Get to know someone new.
- ☐ Invite a coworker to lunch.
- ☐ Start or join a Bible study.
- ☐ Reach out to an old friend.
- ☐ Have a coffee with friends.

Build Up Your Tribe Socially

Social:

WEDNESDAY
WEDNESDAY
WEDNESDAY
WEDNESDAY
WEDNESDAY
WEDNESDAY
WEDNESDAY
WEDNESDAY
WEDNESDAY
WEDNESDAY
WEDNESDAY
WINS
WEDNESDAY
WEDNESDAY
WEDNESDAY
WEDNESDAY

WEDNESDAY

WINS: VICTORY

Celebrate something you have accomplished this week. You can't move on to Thursday without celebrating Wednesday. What have you done that needs applause? Additionally, what will you work towards next? You have done and will continue to do great things. Go celebrate! Yes, you need to celebrate YOU. It's your day. Break out the balloons and pull out all the stops.

WEDNESDAY WINS: VICTORY

Let this choice become your lifestyle—winning will look great on you.

WHAT DID YOU LEARN FROM CHAPTER TWO, "SMALL WINS?"

_____

_____

_____

_____

_____

_____

_____

_____

_____

_____

_____

_____

_____

_____

_____

_____

Find something small to celebrate. Remember, the domino analogy? Small wins lead to bigger wins, but you have to celebrate along the way. Celebration will become your greatest motivator. Good things are happening right now. Don't wait until all your dreams come true before you enjoy the cake!

WHEN WAS THE LAST TIME YOU CELEBRATED YOURSELF FOR A JOB WELL DONE? WHAT DID YOU DO AND WHAT WAS YOUR REWARD?

WEDNESDAY WINS: VICTORY

Let this choice become your lifestyle—winning will look great on you.

YOU SHOULD BE WINNING EVERY WEEK. AVOID THESE SETBACKS THAT WILL ROB YOU OF JOY. IDENTIFY WHAT CATEGORY YOU FALL INTO AND WHY.

1. FORGETTING TO SET GOALS.

2. SETTING THE BAR TOO HIGH.

3. MOVING ON TO THE NEXT GOAL (WITHOUT CELEBRATION).

KEEP WINNING. WRITE DOWN A NEW GOAL AND THE REWARD YOU WILL RECEIVE ONCE IT IS ACCOMPLISHED.

WEDNESDAY WINS: VICTORY

Let this choice become your lifestyle—winning will look great on you.

DAVID WAS A MAN AFTER GOD'S OWN HEART. WHAT PART OF DAVID'S STORY DO YOU IDENTIFY WITH MOST?

_____

_____

_____

_____

_____

_____

_____

_____

_____

_____

_____

_____

_____

_____

_____

HOW DO YOU CELEBRATE GOD'S GOODNESS?

_____

_____

_____

_____

_____

_____

HOW DO YOU BEST CONNECT WITH GOD? (PRAYER, SCRIPTURE, SERVING, NATURE, ETC.)

_____

_____

_____

_____

_____

_____

_____

_____

WEDNESDAY WINS: VICTORY

Let this choice become your lifestyle—winning will look great on you.

PHYSICAL. Treat yourself—no guilt allowed. You need tangible ways of celebrating to associate hard work with reward. Who doesn't like a standing ovation? I bet you have earned one!

NAME ALL THE WAYS YOU COULD CELEBRATE A GREAT WIN. REMEMBER THE STORY OF THE LOUIE PURSE. YOU DETERMINE YOUR PRIZE.

_____

_____

_____

_____

_____

_____

_____

_____

_____

WEDNESDAY WINS: VICTORY

Let this choice become your lifestyle—winning will look great on you.

MENTAL. You need to applaud yourself because you can't rely on other people to celebrate your wins. Mentally allow your wins to soak in, so that you can get excited about what party you will throw for yourself next.

CREATE A PEP TALK THAT YOU WILL RECITE EVERY TIME YOU ARE WORKING TOWARDS A GOAL. YOU GOT THIS!

_____

_____

_____

_____

_____

_____

_____

_____

WEDNESDAY WINS: VICTORY

Let this choice become your lifestyle—winning will look great on you.

EMOTIONAL. Joy is a natural emotion to winning. Children are professionals at jumping up and down to celebrate their success. Consider allowing your inner child to celebrate. Chances are, they will do a better job at it than your adult self.

WHAT PREVENTS YOU FROM CELEBRATING? (DISTRACTIONS, GUILT, FINANCES, ETC.)

_____

_____

_____

_____

_____

_____

_____

_____

_____

_____

WEDNESDAY WINS: VICTORY

Let this choice become your lifestyle—winning will look great on you.

SPIRITUAL. Don't forget to worship God for His faithfulness and the victories He helps you accomplish. Take time to show your gratitude to the one who gives you strength. Your wins are so much greater than yourself.

DO YOU TAKE TIME TO GIVE GOD THANKS FOR YOUR WINS? WHY OR WHY NOT?

_____

_____

_____

_____

_____

_____

_____

_____

_____

_____

WEDNESDAY WINS: VICTORY

Let this choice become your lifestyle—winning will look great on you.

SOCIAL. Tell someone you are winning. Sure, it might feel like bragging but your joy might be contagious. Celebrate with those who will love and appreciate how awesome you are. Some people might be jealous, but others will rejoice alongside you. Find those people. Guess what? You might just encourage someone else to celebrate their wins.

WHO IS ONE PERSON YOU CAN SHARE YOUR WINS WITH?

In what ways can you inspire others to chase their dreams?

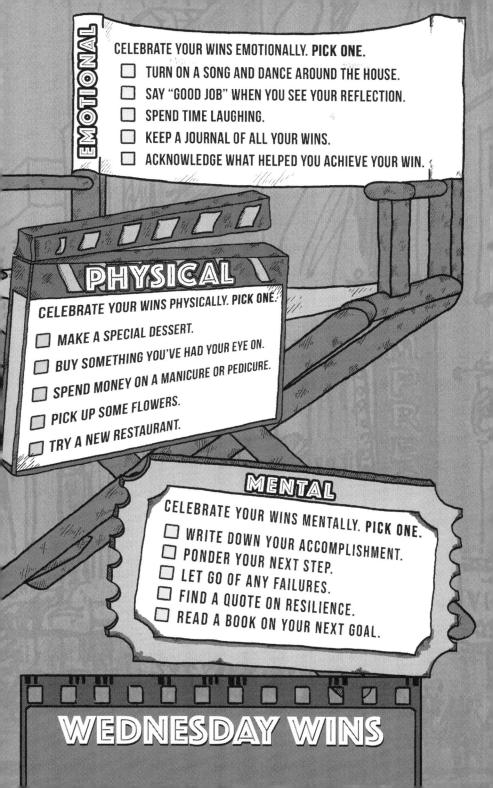

THURSDAY

THURSDAY

THURSDAY

THURSDAY

THURSDAY

THURSDAY

THURSDAY

THURSDAY

THURSDAY

THURSDAY

THURSDAY

THRILLS

THURSDAY

THURSDAY

THURSDAY

THURSDAY

THURSDAY | THRILLS: BRIDGES

THURSDAY

THRILLS: BRIDGES

Bridge moments are opportunities that present themselves to you, daring you to leave what is comfortable behind. You've been waiting to be brave, and Thursday is the day to make it happen! Think of something you have been avoiding. How will you begin to cross that bridge today? You deserve a thrill.

Get your heart racing as you make a date every Thursday to be brave. Remember, bridges can be scary but exhilaration will come once they are crossed. Don't allow fear to stop you. Today is the day to move forward.

Thursday Thrills: Bridges

Bridges connect where you are to where you need to go.

What did you learn from Chapter Seven, "Bridge Moments?"

_____

_____

_____

_____

_____

_____

_____

_____

_____

_____

_____

_____

_____

_____

_____

When you choose to become the bravest version of yourself, you experience tremendous joy. Stepping out of your comfort zone means you explore uncharted territories that take you to new and exciting places.

IDENTIFY ONE BRIDGE THAT YOU NEED TO CROSS.

_____

_____

_____

_____

_____

NAME A TIME YOU CROSSED A SCARY BRIDGE. WHAT HAPPENED?

_____

_____

_____

_____

_____

_____

_____

THURSDAY THRILLS: BRIDGES

Bridges connect where you are to where you need to go.

WHAT STOPS YOU FROM BEING BRAVE? HOW CAN YOU CONQUER THIS FEAR?

_____

_____

_____

_____

_____

Answer the following questions from Chapter 7:

DO I VOLUNTARILY LEAP ENOUGH IN MY LIFE?

_____

_____

_____

_____

_____

_____

DO I BRAVELY BOUNCE BACK?

DO I TAKE RISKS THAT REQUIRE FAITH?

THURSDAY THRILLS: BRIDGES

Bridges connect where you are to where you need to go.

HOW DO YOU RELATE TO PETER'S STORY? WHAT DOES FOLLOWING JESUS LOOK LIKE TO YOU?

_____

_____

_____

_____

_____

_____

_____

_____

_____

_____

_____

_____

_____

_____

⊕

_____

NAME ONE CHANGE YOU NEED TO MAKE THIS YEAR. HOW WILL YOU START? LIST OUT AS MANY STEPS AS YOU CAN THINK OF.

THURSDAY THRILLS: BRIDGES

Bridges connect where you are to where you need to go.

PHYSICAL. Face your fears by taking the first step. Remember the story about Neil Armstrong and how a step can change everything? Define your first step, knowing that you will be closer to the other side by taking action.

EXPLAIN ONE FEAR YOU HAVE AND HOW YOU WILL FACE IT.

_____

_____

_____

_____

_____

_____

_____

_____

_____

_____

Thursday Thrills: Bridges

Bridges connect where you are to where you need to go.

MENTAL. Accept your strength. Your mind might be stopping your heart from moving forward in the needed direction. Don't focus on your past failures because you are far more capable than you think. You are resilient. Go ahead and give yourself a good pep talk. You really can do whatever it is you have been afraid of.

THINK ABOUT A PAST MISTAKE. NAME ALL THE LESSONS LEARNED ALONG THE WAY.

_____

_____

_____

_____

_____

_____

_____

_____

_____

THURSDAY THRILLS: BRIDGES

Bridges connect where you are to where you need to go.

EMOTIONAL. Don't stunt your growth by allowing fear to win. Adventure lies ahead. When your emotions take over, focus on the joy that will come from being brave and making a change. If something goes wrong along the way, give yourself grace and learn from it.

THINK OF SOMETHING YOU WOULD LIKE TO CHANGE. WHAT EMOTIONS MIGHT STOP YOU FROM PURSUING THIS?

_____

_____

_____

_____

_____

_____

_____

_____

_____

_____

THURSDAY THRILLS: BRIDGES

Bridges connect where you are to where you need to go.

SPIRITUAL. Allow faith to be your greatest asset as you walk across your bridge. Remember that God will guide you as you seek His help. If you feel overwhelmed, know that you are never alone. Crossing bridge after bridge will become easier when you trust the one who is leading the way.

WRITE DOWN A PRAYER ASKING GOD FOR STRENGTH TO BE BRAVE.

_____

_____

_____

_____

_____

_____

_____

_____

_____

THURSDAY THRILLS: BRIDGES

Bridges connect where you are to where you need to go.

SOCIAL. Accept support from the people you trust as you brave your endeavor. The bridge is yours to cross, but people are a great resource for encouragement. Choose a partner to keep you accountable. Keep going!

WHAT PARTS OF YOUR JOURNEY WILL BE IMPORTANT FOR YOU TO SHARE? WHY?

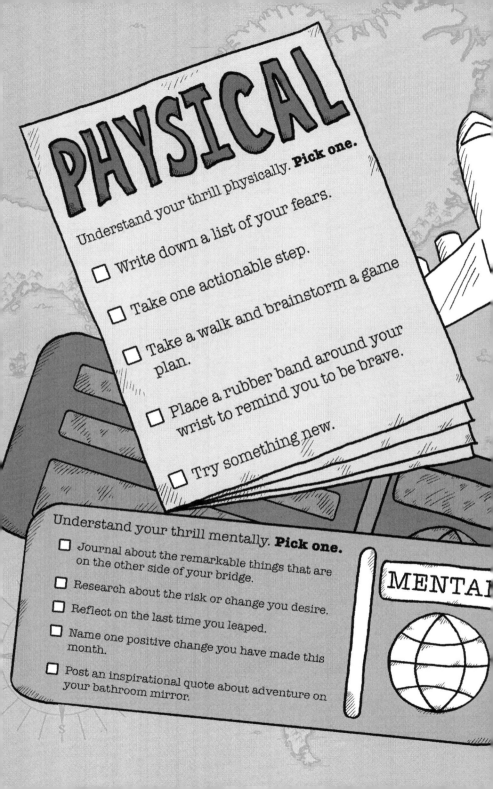

PHYSICAL

Understand your thrill physically. **Pick one.**

- ☐ Write down a list of your fears.
- ☐ Take one actionable step.
- ☐ Take a walk and brainstorm a game plan.
- ☐ Place a rubber band around your wrist to remind you to be brave.
- ☐ Try something new.

Understand your thrill mentally. **Pick one.**

- ☐ Journal about the remarkable things that are on the other side of your bridge.
- ☐ Research about the risk or change you desire.
- ☐ Reflect on the last time you leaped.
- ☐ Name one positive change you have made this month.
- ☐ Post an inspirational quote about adventure on your bathroom mirror.

MENTAL

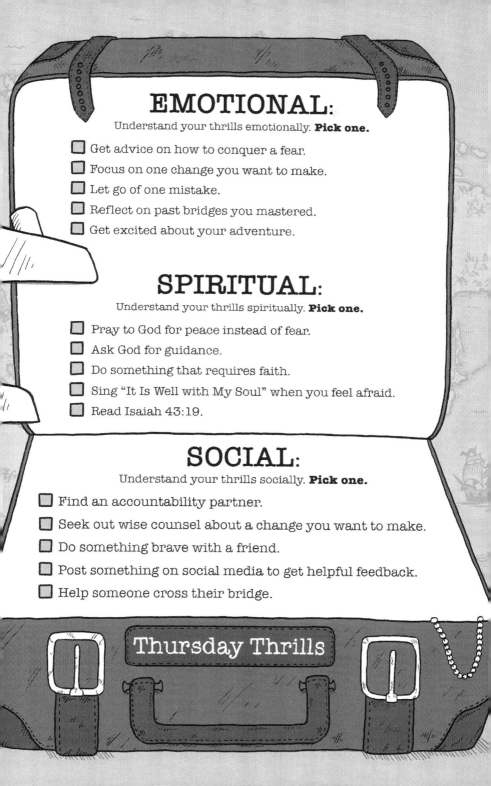

EMOTIONAL:

Understand your thrills emotionally. **Pick one.**

- ☐ Get advice on how to conquer a fear.
- ☐ Focus on one change you want to make.
- ☐ Let go of one mistake.
- ☐ Reflect on past bridges you mastered.
- ☐ Get excited about your adventure.

SPIRITUAL:

Understand your thrills spiritually. **Pick one.**

- ☐ Pray to God for peace instead of fear.
- ☐ Ask God for guidance.
- ☐ Do something that requires faith.
- ☐ Sing "It Is Well with My Soul" when you feel afraid.
- ☐ Read Isaiah 43:19.

SOCIAL:

Understand your thrills socially. **Pick one.**

- ☐ Find an accountability partner.
- ☐ Seek out wise counsel about a change you want to make.
- ☐ Do something brave with a friend.
- ☐ Post something on social media to get helpful feedback.
- ☐ Help someone cross their bridge.

Thursday Thrills

FRIDAY

FRIDAY

FRIDAY

FRIDAY

FRIDAY

FRIDAY

FRIDAY

FRIDAY

FRIDAY

FRIDAY

FRIDAY

FOCUS

FRIDAY

FRIDAY

FRIDAY

FRIDAY

FRIDAY

FOCUS: NON-NEGOTIABLES

The weekend is right around the corner, so make Friday count. As you wrap up the week by sending last minute emails, allow your Friday to be focused. How? Your non-negotiables are waiting on you! What values have you set in stone (your non-negotiables) and what boundaries have you created? Friday is the perfect day to review. What you are doing well and what you can do better?

Friday Focus: Non-Negotiables

Setting non-negotiables requires dedication.

What did you learn from Chapter Three, "Setting Non-Negotiables?"

_____

_____

_____

_____

_____

_____

_____

_____

_____

_____

_____

_____

_____

_____

When it comes to defining your non-negotiables, start with the basics. What are your deal breakers? What do you refuse to tolerate? Begin by listing these things. Having clarity will ensure your success.

WRITE DOWN THREE NON-NEGOTIABLES YOU WILL SET IN STONE. THEY CAN BE PERSONAL, RELATIONAL, SPIRITUAL, ETC.

Friday Focus: Non-Negotiables

Setting non-negotiables requires dedication.

Who do you need to discuss your non-negotiables with?

_____

_____

_____

_____

_____

How will sharing your non-negotiables help keep you accountable in this process?

_____

_____

_____

_____

_____

_____

SHARE ONE PRINCIPLE THAT YOU WILL FIGHT FOR WHEN IT COMES TO YOUR FAITH? REMEMBER THE STORY OF DANIEL.

Friday Focus: Non-Negotiables

Setting non-negotiables requires dedication.

Name one boundary you need to set. This can be personal, relational, spiritual, etc.

_____

_____

_____

_____

_____

Can you think of someone you know who models non-negotiables well in his/her life? What do you think the benefits are?

_____

_____

_____

_____

_____

THINKING BACK TO THE COIN ANALOGY, WHAT IS SOMETHING YOU NEED TO THRIVE?

_____

_____

_____

_____

_____

_____

_____

NOW TO THE FLIP SIDE OF THE COIN, WHAT IS SOMETHING YOU NEED TO AVOID?

_____

_____

_____

_____

_____

_____

_____

FRIDAY FOCUS: NON-NEGOTIABLES

Setting non-negotiables requires dedication.

PHYSICAL. Your non-negotiables need to jump off the page. What do I mean by this? You have to practice them in tangible ways. It's okay to say "NO" to anything that threatens the boundaries you've created. Put reminders in your phone, on your bathroom mirror or inside your Bible to remind you of their importance.

WRITE DOWN A FEW THINGS YOU NEED TO PHYSICALLY SAY "NO" TO. WHERE WILL YOU PUT THESE REMINDERS?

_____

_____

_____

_____

_____

_____

_____

_____

_____

Friday Focus: Non-Negotiables

Setting non-negotiables requires dedication.

Mental. Your non-negotiables need your brain power. They require your consideration. This often starts by thinking about your non-negotiables and developing a mental plan to put them into action. A plan helps you pay attention to what you need to do, in order to stick to your non-negotiables.

Explain why you need to be firm in the three non-negotiables you set.

_____

_____

_____

_____

_____

_____

_____

_____

_____

FRIDAY FOCUS: NON-NEGOTIABLES

Setting non-negotiables requires dedication.

EMOTIONAL. Stay in tune with your feelings as they relate to your non-negotiables. If these emotions are guilt driven or negative, release them. Remain positive, knowing that your non-negotiables will make you better at loving yourself and others. Remember the instruction a flight attendant gives: put on your oxygen mask before assisting others. Just breathe. You got this!

HOW WILL YOU FEEL WHEN YOUR NON-NEGOTIABLES ARE NO LONGER UP FOR GRABS?

_____

_____

_____

_____

_____

_____

_____

WHAT DOES THE BEST CASE SCENARIO LOOK LIKE?

FRIDAY FOCUS: NON-NEGOTIABLES

Setting non-negotiables requires dedication.

SPIRITUAL. Non-negotiables are important especially when it comes to your faith. Nothing is more important than having strong convictions. Know what you believe and never waiver from God's truth. Focus your Friday on spending time with God, asking Him to take you deeper in your walk.

HOW CAN PRAYER, WORSHIP OR READING GOD'S WORD HELP YOU IN STANDING FIRM IN YOUR NON-NEGOTIABLES?

_____

_____

_____

_____

_____

_____

_____

_____

_____

FRIDAY FOCUS: NON-NEGOTIABLES

Setting non-negotiables requires dedication.

SOCIAL. What happens when you set non-negotiables? Your non-negotiables might affect others as you set boundaries. What if some of the people around you push back? Don't let that affect what you have already defined for yourself. Clearly communicating your non-negotiables will reaffirm the commitments you have made.

HOW WILL YOU RESPOND TO SOMEONE WHO DISAGREES WITH YOUR NON-NEGOTIABLES?

_____

_____

_____

_____

_____

_____

_____

_____

MENTAL:

Maximize your focus mentally. Pick one.

☐ Write down one sacrifice you will need to make for your non-negotiables.

☐ Read an article on boundaries.

☐ Imagine what sticking to your non-negotiables will look like.

☐ Remove one obstacle that stands in your way.

☐ Let go of someone who is unsupportive.

PHYSICAL:

Maximize your focus physically. Pick one.

☐ Say "no" to something that threatens your non-negotiables.

☐ Write down three non-negotiables and place them somewhere you can see them.

☐ Order your non-negotiables from highest value to lowest value.

☐ Practice communicating your non-negotiables in the mirror.

☐ Take a field trip to a museum and identify people who stood their ground.

EMOTIONAL:

Maximize your focus emotionally. Pick one.

☐ Write down one guilty thought and put a line through it.

☐ Forgive someone who compromised one of your non-negotiables.

☐ Forgive yourself for compromising on one of your non-negotiables.

☐ Dig deeper into the "why" behind one of your non-negotiables.

☐ Remember a previous moment where a non-negotiable brought you joy and write it down.

SOCIAL:

Maximize your focus socially. **Pick one.**

☐ Ask a friend to keep you accountable.

☐ Share a non-negotiable with someone who will be affected by it.

☐ Encourage a friend or family member to create their own non-negotiables.

☐ Share an inspirational story on social media about a person who stood for their convictions.

☐ Compliment and thank someone who has assisted you in maintaining your non-negotiables.

SPIRITUAL:

Maximize your focus spiritually. **Pick one.**

☐ Name one specific area you need more faith.

☐ Ask the Holy Spirit to increase your conviction.

☐ Write out a personal faith statement.

☐ Memorize the Ten Commandments (God's non-negotiables). These can be found in Exodus 20:2–17 and Deuteronomy 5:6–21.

☐ Read Romans 12:2.
   "Don't copy the behavior and customs of this world, but let God transform you into a new person by changing the way you think. Then you will learn to know God's will for you, which is good and pleasing and perfect."

Friday Focus

SATURDAY
SATURDAY
SATURDAY
SATURDAY
SATURDAY
SATURDAY
SATURDAY
SATURDAY
SATURDAY
SATURDAY
SATURDAY

SMILES

SATURDAY
SATURDAY
SATURDAY
SATURDAY

SATURDAY

SMILES: GIVING

It's Saturday! Chances are, you will be in contact with new people. You might find yourself going through a drive-thru for a quick meal, stopping by your favorite coffee spot or browsing through the aisles of a shopping store. The point? You have opportunities to give. Whether you extend a compliment or donate your time to someone in need, you have endless options to create joy. Put a smile on someone's face because today is about giving back.

Saturday Smiles: Giving

God blesses us so we can bless others.

What did you learn from Chapter Five, "The Golden Gift?"

_____

_____

_____

_____

_____

_____

_____

_____

_____

_____

_____

_____

_____

_____

_____

_____

Giving can be a joyful endeavor when you choose to give meaningful gifts instead of presents. Allow your hands and heart to be open to the practice of giving. When you give, you recognize just how much you have! How can you become a cheerful giver? Let's reflect on this together by focusing one day a week on giving.

WHEN WAS THE LAST TIME YOU GAVE A MEANINGFUL GIFT? WHAT WAS THE GIFT AND WHO WAS THE RECIPIENT?

SATURDAY SMILES: GIVING

God blesses us so we can bless others.

THINK BACK TO THE STORY OF WHEN MY MOTHER GAVE AWAY HER NEW SENSA PEN. HAVE YOU EVER GIVEN AWAY SOMETHING YOU LOVED? WHAT HAPPENED?

_____

_____

_____

_____

_____

_____

_____

_____

_____

_____

_____

RE-READ MATTHEW 6:30.

"BUT WHEN YOU GIVE TO SOMEONE IN NEED, DON'T LET YOUR LEFT HAND KNOW WHAT YOUR RIGHT HAND IS DOING."

BASED ON THE PIANO ANALOGY, IN REFERENCE TO THIS VERSE, WHAT CHALLENGES MIGHT PREVENT YOU FROM GIVING FREELY?

_____

_____

_____

_____

_____

_____

_____

_____

_____

_____

SATURDAY SMILES: GIVING

God blesses us so we can bless others.

WHAT ARE SOME TAKEAWAYS FROM THE WIDOW'S STORY IN THE BIBLE?

_____

_____

_____

_____

_____

_____

HOW DO YOU SACRIFICE SOME OF THE THINGS YOU HAVE FOR GOD'S GLORY? THIS COULD BE YOUR TIME, TALENTS, RESOURCES, ETC.

_____

_____

_____

_____

_____

IMAGINE YOU HAD ONE HUNDRED DOLLARS TO GIVE AWAY. WHERE WOULD YOU GO AND WHO WOULD YOU GIVE IT TO?

Saturday Smiles: Giving

God blesses us so we can bless others.

Physical. Tangible gifts can express gratitude toward others. Give a gift instead of a present. How will you be intentional about giving a meaningful gift? Blessing someone with no strings attached is always a beautiful act.

How can you bless someone today? Be creative.

_____

_____

_____

_____

_____

_____

_____

_____

_____

Saturday Smiles: Giving

God blesses us so we can bless others.

Mental. Did you know that giving can be a mental exercise? Think of how you have been blessed and make a gratitude list. Then, ponder how you can bless someone else out of your abundance. Like playing the piano, it takes practice to master giving.

Write down all the things you have been blessed with. This will be your gratitude list to refer to any time you are feeling upset. You are blessed!

_____

_____

_____

_____

_____

_____

_____

_____

_____

Saturday Smiles: Giving

God blesses us so we can bless others.

EMOTIONAL. I guarantee that if you allow your heart to participate in the practice of giving, you will be amazed at the results. Your joy will bubble up! Don't hold onto the things you have too tightly. Instead, allow yourself to let go. Remember, you are a blessing.

MAKE A LIST OF ALL THE PEOPLE WHO HAVE BLESSED YOU OVER THE PAST YEAR. HOW DID THIS MAKE YOU FEEL?

SATURDAY SMILES: GIVING

God blesses us so we can bless others.

SPIRITUAL. Have you thanked God for all that He has done for you? Your joy will multiply once you remember all the ways He has blessed you. If it has been a while since you showed gratitude, take the time to respond to His goodness today.

WRITE DOWN A PRAYER, PSALM OR POEM OF THANKSGIVING TO GOD.

_____

_____

_____

_____

_____

_____

_____

_____

_____

SATURDAY SMILES: GIVING

God blesses us so we can bless others.

SOCIAL. Find people who will join you in giving. I guarantee a tribe member will be thrilled if you ask them to contribute to the joy of giving back. Make it a fun Saturday challenge as you brainstorm ideas on how you can give together. You will be surprised at the outcome. Food pantries, clothing drives and homeless shelters were born from generous givers.

THINK OF A CAUSE THAT GIVES BACK. HOW CAN YOU FIND OUT MORE INFORMATION AND GET VOLUNTEERS TO HELP?

_____

_____

_____

_____

_____

_____

_____

_____

PHYSICAL:

Share a smile physically. Pick one.

- ☐ Find a sentimental gift for someone (not a present).
- ☐ Donate clothes or food to a shelter.
- ☐ Pay for someone's coffee order.
- ☐ Send a handwritten thank-you letter to someone.
- ☐ Give a sincere compliment.

MENTAL:

Share a smile mentally. Pick one.

- ☐ Make a list of precious keepsakes you have received.
- ☐ Identify one of the most generous people you know, and think about what makes them that way.
- ☐ Adjust your budget for blessing others.
- ☐ Discover your tribe's favorite gift ideas.
- ☐ Memorize important dates or anniversaries for your loved ones.

EMOTIONAL:

Share a smile emotionally. Pick one.

- ☐ Practice joyful giving by smiling as you give.
- ☐ Give the gift of laughter. Make someone laugh today.
- ☐ Recall a special gift you have received and why it is meaningful.
- ☐ Thank someone who sacrificed something for you.
- ☐ Create a gift from the heart for someone.

SPIRITUAL:

Share a smile spiritually. **Pick one.**

☐ Make a gratitude list of good things that have happened this past week.

☐ Ask God for a generous heart.

☐ Give a Bible to someone.

☐ Give more than your tithe as an offering to God.

☐ Read 2 Corinthians 9:7.
> "Each of you should give what you have decided in your heart to give, not reluctantly or under compulsion, for God loves a cheerful giver."

SOCIAL:

Share a smile socially. **Pick one.**

☐ Leave a generous tip for your server.

☐ Help someone who is in need.

☐ Ask a friend to volunteer with you locally.

☐ Start an online fundraiser for a cause you care about.

☐ Give your time to someone needing mentorship.

Saturday Smiles

SUNDAY

SUNDAY

SUNDAY

SUNDAY

SUNDAY

SUNDAY

SUNDAY

SUNDAY

SUNDAY

SUNDAY

SUNDAY

SHIFT

SUNDAY

SUNDAY

SUNDAY

SUNDAY

SUNDAY

SHIFT: HOPE

Sunday offers hope. You may find yourself praising God at church in the morning or rooting for your favorite sports team on the couch in the afternoon. We all need hope. But, we have options as to what we put our hope in. Start today by putting your hope in God. Dedicate an entire day to shift your thoughts from despair to hope. This will change your Sunday and your entire week. Hope is available to you today.

SUNDAY SHIFT: HOPE

Hope allows joy to sustain our hearts, even when pain pierces through.

WHAT DID YOU LEARN FROM CHAPTER SIX, "BLEACHED WHITE HOPE?"

✝

Tragedy can be an unlikely opportunity where hope can arise. Hope is found in Jesus and through faith in the sacrifice that He made on the cross. As you take time to heal and reflect on your story, allow God to write the next chapter.

WHAT LIFE EVENTS CAUSED YOU PAIN?

_____

_____

_____

_____

_____

WHAT HELPED YOU THROUGH?

_____

_____

_____

_____

_____

_____

_____

Sunday Shift: Hope

Hope allows joy to sustain our hearts, even when pain pierces through.

Reflect on a time when you were hurt, angry or disappointed with God.

_____

_____

_____

_____

_____

_____

_____

_____

_____

_____

_____

_____

_____

_____ ✝ _____

AS YOU REFLECTED ON A TIME WHERE YOU WERE HURT, DID YOU FIND HOPE AND EXPERIENCE HEALING? WHY OR WHY NOT?

Sunday Shift: Hope

Hope allows joy to sustain our hearts, even when pain pierces through.

Re-read Hebrews 12:2.

"… Because of the joy awaiting him, he endured the cross, disregarding its shame. Now he is seated in the place of honor beside God's throne."

Do you think that pain and joy can exist at the same time?

_____

_____

_____

_____

_____

_____

_____

_____

_____

_____

✝

WHAT DOES THE CROSS MEAN TO YOU?

Sunday Shift: Hope

Hope allows joy to sustain our hearts, even when pain pierces through.

Physical. Experiencing joy while you are hurting can seem impossible. While you cannot live a pain-free life, you can reclaim the joy that's been missing. Think about it this way, Jesus endured the horrific pain of the cross for the joy of knowing and saving you.

Think back to a time where you were in pain and experienced God's healing. How does this serve as a reminder that God is your source of hope?

_____

_____

_____

_____

_____

_____

_____

_____ ✝ _____

Sunday Shift: Hope

Hope allows joy to sustain our hearts, even when pain pierces through.

Mental. Your mind is often the place where the pain replays itself. Letting go of the pain means no longer focusing on the hurt but trusting in the healer. Jesus wants to replace your pain with a joy that He promises comes in the morning. Do you trust Him to heal your heartache?

Share a painful memory. What is the next step needed for you to receive God's healing power?

_____

_____

_____

_____

_____

_____

_____

_____

_____ ✝ _____

_____

_____

_____

_____

_____

_____

_____

_____

_____

_____

_____

_____

_____

_____

_____

_____

_____ ✝ _____

Sunday Shift: Hope

Hope allows joy to sustain our hearts, even when pain pierces through.

EMOTIONAL. Negative emotions can hit you without warning. Don't let them get the best of you. You can rise up even after the greatest storms. God promises to never leave you, even when your emotions tell you otherwise.

SHIFT YOUR EMOTIONS RIGHT NOW. FOCUS ON A TIME WHEN YOU EXPERIENCED PURE JOY. WHAT HAPPENED?

_____

_____

_____

_____

_____

_____

_____

_____

_____

_____ ✝ _____

AFTER FOCUSING ON A JOYFUL EXPERIENCE, HOW DOES THIS ENCOURAGE YOU THAT HAPPINESS IS STILL AHEAD?

Sunday Shift: Hope

Hope allows joy to sustain our hearts, even when pain pierces through.

SPIRITUAL. God is the only one who can truly heal your heart. Any other solutions will only serve as a temporary fix. How do you give everything over to God and trust that He will not leave you broken? He does His best work even when you are at your worst.

WHAT DO YOU NEED HEALING FROM?

_____

_____

_____

_____

_____

_____

_____

_____

_____

_____ ✝ _____

CAN YOU TRUST GOD? WHY OR WHY NOT?

SUNDAY SHIFT: HOPE

Hope allows joy to sustain our hearts, even when pain pierces through.

SOCIAL. Never underestimate the power of other people standing beside you when you have fallen. God will bring you the right people when you need them most. Sometimes it only takes one person to help build you back up after your world has been shattered. Have you experienced this truth yet? I pray you have.

WHO HAS BEEN THERE FOR YOU TIME AND TIME AGAIN? HOW CAN YOU BE LIKE THAT PERSON FOR SOMEONE WHO IS HURTING?

✝

_____

_____

_____

_____

_____

_____

_____

_____

_____

_____

_____

_____

_____

_____

_____

_____ ✝ _____

PHYSICAL

Begin to shift physically. **Pick one.**

☐ Place a small cross somewhere you can see it.

☐ Speak God's promises out loud.

☐ Bleach something.

☐ Write a message of hope to a stranger and leave it in a public place.

☐ Look for beauty throughout the day.

MENTAL

Begin to shift mentally. **Pick one.**

☐ Meditate on the Psalms and journal about them.

☐ Read a topical book on hope.

☐ List a few things that bring you hope.

☐ Sit outside and be still.

☐ Live in the present, instead of the past.

EMOTIONAL

Begin to shift emotionally. **Pick one.**

☐ Write down a joyful memory.

☐ Speak to a professional grief counselor.

☐ Study the seven stages of grief.

☐ Cry or laugh.

☐ Process one painful moment.

Sunday Shift

SOCIAL
Begin to shift socially. **Pick one.**

☐ Bring a friend to church.

☐ Share your story of hope with someone.

☐ Donate your time to a women's shelter.

☐ Ask a stranger if they need prayer.

☐ Meet a physical need of hunger.

SPIRITUAL
Begin to shift spiritually. **Pick one.**

☐ Pray for the Holy Spirit's comfort.

☐ Praise God through the heartbreak.

☐ Thank God for your prosperous, hopeful future.

☐ Take communion and remember the cross.

☐ Read Romans 15:13.
"I pray that God, the source of hope, will fill you completely with joy and peace because you trust in him. Then you will overflow with confident hope through the power of the Holy Spirit."

ADDITIONAL NOTES

THE END? It's hard for me to say that this workbook is officially completed.

WRITE DOWN ANY FINAL THOUGHTS YOU HAVE ON ANY OF THE CHAPTERS.

_____

_____

_____

_____

_____

_____

_____

_____

_____

_____

_____ ✝ _____

WHAT ARE THE MOST IMPORTANT THINGS YOU WILL COMMIT TO TRY?

_____

_____

_____

_____

_____

_____

_____

_____

_____

_____

_____

I know you will do great things and I can't wait to hear all about them.

Love, Daira

ACKNOWLEDGMENTS
ACKNOWLEDGMENTS
ACKNOWLEDGMENTS
ACKNOWLEDGMENTS
ACKNOWLEDGMENTS
ACKNOWLEDGMENTS
ACKNOWLEDGMENTS
ACKNOWLEDGMENTS
ACKNOWLEDGMENTS
ACKNOWLEDGMENTS
ACKNOWLEDGMENTS

PEOPLE I LOVE

ACKNOWLEDGMENTS
ACKNOWLEDGMENTS
ACKNOWLEDGMENTS
ACKNOWLEDGMENTS

ACKNOWLEDGMENTS

PEOPLE I LOVE

First and foremost, thank you Jesus for being faithful and allowing my heart to be spilled out on every page. You make me brave.

Sean, you are like the perfect summer day—anyone who meets you says "hello" to sunshine. How am I this blessed to call you my daily ray of light? I am so in love with you. You are my happiest thought, my greatest gem and my truest love. You will always embody what joy looks like to me in human form—thank you for giving me a front row seat.

Mom, thank you for spending countless hours helping me edit all my thoughts. You always know what I mean to say! You are such an endless treasure chest for me—priceless in knowledge and love. I hope someday I am as extraordinary as you are.

Dad, thank you for instilling confidence within me from a young age. You always see me at my best, even when

I am still a long way off. You are a reflection of God's heart—what more could a daughter ever ask for? You will always be my first love.

Alex, someday we will eat the cheesiest pizza and cruise around listening to the loudest music again. I can hardly wait. Until then, dance the streets of heaven for me with every ounce of joy that I always saw within you.

Kelli, you have walked beside me on this exciting journey, bringing clarity and encouragement every step of the way. I am blessed to call you my editor and friend.

Galina, thank you for bringing my stories to life with your beautiful illustrations. Your uncanny ability to capture each word made it feel as though you were there when it happened.

Last but never least, a sincere thank you to everyone who is mentioned in the stories throughout this honest to goodness joyful journey of mine. Each of you are like sprinkles to my hot fudge sundae. I couldn't have written my joy down without you. Literally!

ABOUT THE AUTHOR
ABOUT THE AUTHOR
ABOUT THE AUTHOR
ABOUT THE AUTHOR
ABOUT THE AUTHOR
ABOUT THE AUTHOR
ABOUT THE AUTHOR
ABOUT THE AUTHOR
ABOUT THE AUTHOR
ABOUT THE AUTHOR
ABOUT THE AUTHOR

DAIRA AVERY TRAYNOR

ABOUT THE AUTHOR
ABOUT THE AUTHOR
ABOUT THE AUTHOR
ABOUT THE AUTHOR

ABOUT THE AUTHOR

DAIRA AVERY TRAYNOR

Daira Avery Traynor well known for her abundant joy is the Girls Minister at First Baptist Dallas. Daira is passionate about helping the next generation of 7th-12th grade girls discovery their true identity in Christ.

She is a graduate of Belmont University in Nashville, Tennessee where she received a degree in Commercial Music. Worship is always at the heartbeat of everything she does.

Daira can best be described as the girl who owns way too many pairs of shoes, turns a stranger into a friend over coffee and cooks endless amounts of pasta for the excuse to have more people around her table.

Daira is a proud Texan who resides with her amazingly funny husband, Sean Traynor, and their dog, Boots.

You can find her wherever the music is playing loudly or teens are gathered.

Made in the USA
Middletown, DE
11 April 2023